1 0 S T E P S T O

Successful Meetings

ASTD

PRESS

Alexandria, Virginia

ASTD Press is an internationally renowned source of insightful and practical information on workplace learning and performance topics, including training basics, evaluation and return-on-investment, instructional systems development, e-learning, leadership, and career development.

Ordering information: Books published by ASTD Press can be purchased by visiting our website at store.astd.org or by calling 800.628.2783 or 703.683.8100.

Library of Congress Control Number: 2008928320
ISBN-10: 1-56286-547-1
ISBN-13: 978-1-56286-547-4

ASTD Press Editorial Staff:
Director: Cat Russo
Manager, Acquisitions and Author Relations: Mark Morrow
Editorial Manager: Jacqueline Edlund-Braun
Senior Associate Editor: Tora Estep
Associate Editor: Maureen Soyars
Writer: Lynn Sparapany Lewis, Learning Solutions, LLC
Copyeditor: Pamela Lankas
Indexer: Mary Kidd
Proofreader: IGS
Interior Design and Production: International Graphics Services
Cover Design: Elizabeth Park

Printed by Victor Graphics, Inc., Baltimore, Maryland,
www.victorgraphics.com

Let's face it, most people spend their days in chaotic, fast-paced, time- and resource-strained organizations. Finding time for just one more project, assignment, or even learning opportunity—no matter how career enhancing or useful—is difficult to imagine. The *10-Steps* series is designed for today's busy professional who needs advice and guidance on a wide array of topics ranging from project management to people management, from business strategy to decision making and time management, from stepping in to deliver a presentation for someone else to researching and creating a compelling presentation as well as effectively delivering the content. Each book in this ASTD series promises to take its readers on a journey to basic understanding, with practical application the ultimate destination. This is truly a just-tell-me-what-to-do-now series. You will find action-driven language teamed with examples, worksheets, case studies, and tools to help you quickly implement the right steps and chart a path to your own success. The *10-Steps* series will appeal to a broad business audience from middle managers to upper-level management. Workplace learning and human resource professionals along with other professionals seeking to improve their value proposition in their organizations will find these books a great resource.

C O N T E N T S

P R E F A C E

At all organizational levels, business professionals are spending more of their time in meetings. So, what's the organizational benefit for all of the time and effort spent in these meetings? Much of that benefit is directly determined by the productivity of the individuals attending the meetings and how successful they are at accomplishing the meeting objectives.

Conducting highly effective and efficient meetings is an essential skill for all business professionals. So, whether your next meeting is a small-group, facilitative session or a global teleconference, the same planning and presentation principles apply.

So how do you go about developing and facilitating an effective, results-oriented meeting? *10 Steps to Successful Meetings* provides the key information you need to accomplish this goal. You can jump to any step in process or start at the beginning. These steps include

1. deciding if a meeting is necessary
2. creating the agenda and identifying participants
3. laying the groundwork for success
4. identifying appropriate meeting facilities
5. using a reliable process to facilitate the meeting
6. building a game plan for success
7. preparing for the meeting
8. conducting the meeting

9. managing difficult situations and participants
10. evaluating success and following up.

10 Steps to Successful Meetings is part of ASTD's *10-Step* series and was written to provide you with a proven process, quick reference tips, and practical worksheets to help you successfully plan and lead any meeting.

INTRODUCTION

Take a moment to think about the most productive meeting that you've attended. What made it productive? Meetings have the potential to bring a group of participants together to act as a brain trust. This group can often have a profound impact on an organization or in crafting the policies or decisions that need to be implemented to better the organization, its processes, or the environment in which employees are expected to perform. With such power possible, a key tenet of productive meetings is that the right people are invited and that their time is used wisely.

Employees at all levels spend a significant portion of their working lives in meetings. The time spent in meeting rooms needs to be effective and goal oriented to offset the time subtracted from individual productivity. Business professionals need to know how to maximize a meeting's usefulness and generate results in the process. Take a minute to estimate the cost for one excessive, non-value-adding meeting that wasted precious time and the organization's resources. How much do you think it cost the organization? Before answering, don't forget to include

◆ estimated hourly salary of each participant

◆ estimated hourly cost of benefits for every individual (some estimate that benefits cost approximately 33 percent of annual salaries)

◆ hourly cost of use of facilities

◆ hourly cost of use of equipment

◆ lost productivity by diverting resources to attend a meeting vs. working on other initiatives.

Got a number in mind? Now multiply that by the number of hours spent in the meeting. That can be a hefty number—especially if the meeting is a weekly or monthly recurring event. Keep in mind that meetings do not have to be a big waste of time and money. Meetings go awry because leaders do not appropriately plan in advance and lack the skills to effectively guide and facilitate the meeting. By following 10 simple steps, you can create meetings that generate excitement, creativity, and innovation and achieve defined goals.

This book, *10 Steps to Successful Meetings*, provides techniques for confirming when a meeting is necessary, offers suggestions on creating and developing an engaging meeting agenda, helps you identify the right participants to invite, supplies techniques for successfully facilitating groups, and offers strategies for handling difficult situations and participants.

Use the key steps in this book as needed. Whether you are leading a status meeting, team kickoffs, strategic-planning sessions, or problem-solving initiatives, the same steps to planning and leading meetings still apply. This book focuses on
◆ deciding if a meeting is necessary
◆ determining which type of meeting is appropriate
◆ creating the meeting agenda and identifying participants to invite
◆ identifying the appropriate meeting location
◆ inviting participants
◆ reviewing techniques to preparing for the meeting
◆ conducting the meeting
◆ managing difficult situations and participants
◆ following up and evaluating success.

Structure of This Book

10 Steps to Successful Meetings will help you to quickly identify the meeting goals and required participants, to develop a detailed meeting agenda, and to lead meetings that effectively accomplish the defined goals and objectives. In particular, this book delves into these steps:

- ◆ **Step 1: Decide If the Meeting Is Necessary**—Because many business professionals spend an extraordinary amount of their working time in meetings, all of this time spent should drive extraordinary results. Excessive, unnecessary meetings are a waste of time for the employee and the organization. Step 1 focuses on how to determine if a meeting is necessary, presents tips for defining meeting objectives, and describes the types of meetings and special considerations for each type.

- ◆ **Step 2: Create the Agenda and Identify Participants**—After determining that a meeting is required, the next step is to identify who needs to be there and what the participants need to do to achieve the business goals and objectives. This step defines the role of a meeting leader, describes how to create a meeting agenda and estimate timing, determines who should attend, defines the team roles, and creates the meeting invitation. Any work assignments that are required prior to attending the meeting are sent at this point as well.

- ◆ **Step 3: Lay the Groundwork for Success**—The next step in the process is to create a meeting agenda. The agenda serves as a blueprint—a master roadmap to navigate the meeting to its final destination, that is, the desired business goals. This step outlines the key components of every meeting: opening, transitions, ground rules, role definitions, how to guide the meeting, use of a parking lot to keep the meeting on track, and techniques for generating discussion.

- ◆ **Step 4: Identify Appropriate Facilities**—No matter how great the agenda and planned activities are, if the meeting room is too hot, too small, or too dark and dreary, then as the meeting leader you will fight an uphill battle to make the meeting productive. This step focuses on planning and setting up the meeting environment to facilitate discussion and idea generation.

◆ **Step 5: Use a Reliable Process to Facilitate the Meeting**—When starting a meeting, it is always important to keep in mind what you are trying to achieve. Depending on the type of meeting, leaders often need to use a variety of facilitation techniques to engage participants to get them to identify problems, generate ideas, and discuss how to implement the most viable solutions. In these cases, meeting leaders assume the role of facilitators and must leverage a different set of skills and activities to guide the group to accomplishing the defined goals. This step focuses on conducting a meeting using a defined set of processes and tools for facilitating groups.

◆ **Step 6: Build a Game Plan for Success**—A hallmark of an effective meeting is sufficient preparation, and that goes for every component of the agenda. This chapter provides tips and techniques to prepare for the meeting, discusses how to finalize and organize your materials, prepares the leader for tricky and difficult questions, and identifies the due diligence necessary to know the audience and plan for difficult situations.

◆ **Step 7: Prepare for the Meeting**—With most meetings, although you probably want to keep presentations to a minimum so that you capitalize on the energy of the group, presenting is still an important way to convey information. This piece of the puzzle reviews presentation techniques, describes various strategies to involve participants, provides guidelines for creating effective visual aids, and reviews tactics for what to do when things go wrong and the meeting gets off track.

◆ **Step 8: Conduct the Meeting**—A productive meeting doesn't necessarily begin when everyone arrives. It begins at the time designated. Once it is time to begin, successful leaders manage meetings skillfully by maintaining a productive environment, sticking to the agenda, encouraging participation, and protecting minority opinions. Step 8 focuses on how to conduct productive meetings; describes the appropriate use of verbal and nonverbal communication, multicultural communication considerations, and gaining agreement; and explains how to conclude the meeting and assign action items to participants.

◆ **Step 9: Manage Difficult Situations and Participants—** Maintaining control of a meeting is much tougher when a participant behaves rudely or inappropriately. The focus here is on strategies for identifying group dysfunction and difficult participants and guidelines on when and how to intervene appropriately and resolve conflicts.

◆ **Step 10: Evaluate Your Success and Follow Up—**Given the amount of time spent in meetings, as a best practice, successful meeting leaders evaluate the meetings they have led to improve future sessions. This step in the process involves measuring the meeting success based on accomplishment of the objectives outlined, if the meeting was held in a timely manner, and if participants were satisfied with the results. Strategies for evaluating the meeting and tools for closing the meeting by distributing meeting notes and keeping track of action items and commitments assigned to participants are detailed.

Review these 10 steps as often as needed to build and perfect your ability to plan and lead effective, interactive, and performance-driven meetings.

Decide If the Meeting Is Necessary

STEP 1.

OVERVIEW

Decide if a meeting is necessary

Define meeting goals and desired outcomes

Types of meetings

At all organizational levels, more and more business professionals are spending time in meetings. Meet some of the typical meeting-goers:

There are the group leaders who call all subordinates into one room—without a clear purpose or agenda defined—and play the meeting master. They are similar to some project managers who relish the temporary chance to chair meetings of their peers. As for the bosses who detest department meetings—they perceive meetings as a waste of time and would rather write their workers a memo because they do not need staff input on decisions. And then there are the workers who agree with the boss. They have more important things to do than sit through a meeting in which their opinions and ideas do not count. There are also the eager meeting attendees. To them, a meeting is a paid break in the day, a chance to catch up on daydreaming, list making, or doodling.

Many of the meeting-goers just described have been jaded by attending too many ineffective meetings that proved to be a waste of time. However, there is a rare group of meeting-goers, group leaders, and project managers with valid, business-oriented reasons for every meeting they call. These individuals demonstrate exceptional skills in conducting and facilitating meetings and achieving the desired outcomes. They recognize the benefits of orally communicating information and soliciting spontaneous feedback from a group. The energy of the meeting, the importance of the dialogue, and the ideas generated are valued by all attendees, who leave feeling positive and motivated by the work accomplished through active participation in the meeting.

Well-organized meetings can produce ideas and solutions to problems that might not occur to one individual working alone at a desk. That is the power of well-planned, highly productive meetings.

Decide If a Meeting Is Necessary

One of the first things to do before sending a meeting invitation is to confirm that a meeting is really the best use of people's time and the organization's resources. Do you need to have a face-to-face or teleconference meeting—or will a quick email convey the same information for all involved to effectively perform their jobs or be updated on a project's status? One golden rule: Only hold a meeting when there is good reason. As a guideline, you should hold a meeting when you want

- ◆ to present information to a lot of people quickly, and you don't want to rewrite it
- ◆ to get input from others regarding ideas
- ◆ to gain "buy in" or ownership for a problem or solution
- ◆ to motivate and energize a team
- ◆ to gain consensus and make decisions.

Other good reasons to hold meetings are planning projects, brainstorming, and problem solving. To help you get started, use Worksheet 1.1 to assess if scheduling a meeting is appropriate.

Define Meeting Goals and Desired Outcomes

Once you've decided that a meeting is in fact needed, the next step is to define the meeting goals and to determine the desired outcomes. A productive meeting begins with a purpose. If you call a meeting, then you need to plan and execute the meeting, always keeping its purpose top of mind. That means that every decision you make—from whom to invite to how to run the meeting—revolves around the meeting's goal.

When crafting the meeting goals and objectives, evaluate them by thinking SMART: Are they specific, measurable, achievable, realistic, and timebound? What outcomes would indicate that the meeting achieved the objectives?

Outcomes define the tangible end products of a meeting—for example, a recommendation, a prioritized list of ideas, or a solution to a problem.

POINTER When crafting the meeting goals and objectives, evaluate them by thinking SMART: Are they specific, measurable, achievable, realistic, and timebound? If they are not, it will be difficult to determine whether the meeting achieved the objectives.

A clearly defined outcome statement is a product—not a process. It should focus on nouns to describe the end result (for example, lists, timelines, solutions to a problem) and yield a set of realistic goals that can be accomplished within the time constraints of the meeting. For example, a meeting objective might be to determine the causes behind the declining sales of X product and to identify at least three viable solutions to the problem. So, having the group brainstorm or generate at least three viable solutions is the stated outcome indicating success for the meeting.

If the purpose of the meeting is murky and not clearly defined, it may not be the appropriate time to hold a meeting. Many times there are efficient alternatives for communicating information—such as sending an email or collaborating electronically on a shared area regarding solutions to a possible problem.

Types of Meetings

When a meeting is necessary, determine which type of meeting approach would best accomplish the defined goals. There are several types of meetings, including new team/project kickoff, informational, problem solving, and facilitative, as well as instructional meetings or training sessions.

New Team/Project Kickoff Meeting

Quite often business professionals need to hold meetings to acquaint and orient a new team to their mission, or to kick off a new project or initiative. Any stumbling during a kickoff meeting often makes participants wary of what's coming next when they get into the thick of the project. These types of meetings are often the first time team members meet each other and discuss the goals of the initiative. So, as a best practice, kickoff of new team meetings should include

- ◆ introduction of the team members
- ◆ a project overview
- ◆ management's expectations of the team
- ◆ time to address participants' concerns or questions
- ◆ drafting team ground rules and perhaps a project charter.

Informational Meeting

When news, plans, or other information needs to be shared with a group, this information is often best communicated orally and with visual aids. Also, some types of individuals need to relate or receive information from other people and have to ask questions to fully comprehend the new material.

Informational meetings are also called to create proper attitudes or, more specifically, to sell the participants on an idea, policy, or decision that needs to be made. If you decide that participants need to be "sold," in general, sending a written memo is not as effective as oral communication. The oral approach offers more opportunity for persuasion. It also offers the flexibility of adjusting to the reaction of the group or when talking with specific individuals. This meeting type also provides an opportunity for repeating significant facts, emphasizing points, overcoming objections, and tailoring the sales approach to the audience or individuals.

Problem-Solving Meeting

A problem-solving meeting has one objective: to solve a problem. Just as the saying goes: "two heads are better than one," this is often the case when gathering a group of people to focus on finding solutions to an issue.

The problem is often one that affects everyone in the group and can best be solved by discussing and debating suspected causes and different points of view. These types of problems run a huge gamut, including customer service catastrophes, production breakdowns, interpersonal conflicts, flat or stagnant sales, low employee motivation and morale, new compensation programs or policies, and so on.

POINTER

If a critical participant is not available to attend a meeting, it may be best to reschedule or postpone the meeting until all of the required, key players can participate.

Another reason to hold problem-solving meetings is that when people are included in the problem-solving process, they develop a sense of ownership and inherently tend to buy-in to the ultimate solution.

Facilitative Meeting

Facilitative meetings, often considered "information-gathering" meetings, can be held for a variety of reasons. Usually, the leader of the meeting wants to gather information or insight from the participants by asking for ideas, reactions, accomplishments, problems, solutions, or other kinds of information. The meeting leader usually leverages a variety of facilitation techniques to actively involve the group, including questioning techniques, idea-generation activities such as brainstorming, and decision-making tools—all of which help the group reach agreement and decide on a plan of action.

Instructional Meetings or Training Sessions

There are many approaches available to train and develop people:
- reading books or articles
- attending correspondence courses
- coaching by the boss or other qualified person
- instructing individuals with or without a computer
- sending individuals to an outside training course
- conducting in-house training meetings.

All of the training approaches, if effective, can improve the knowledge, skill, attitude, and behavior of the trainee. Each has certain advantages and disadvantages related to the cost-benefit ratio.

Here are some of the circumstances that may make an in-house training meeting worthwhile:
- A number of people (a minimum of 10) have common training needs.
- A training meeting can satisfy their needs.
- Qualified instructors are available from inside or outside.

- Good facilities are available for the meetings.
- Time for the participants will be made available by their line managers, or participants will take the training on their own time, or the organization is willing to pay participants for attending on their own time.
- A qualified in-house person is willing and able to spend time to plan and coordinate the meetings.
- The benefits are worth the cost.

Considerations for Virtual Meetings

Assembling and working with virtual teams is common practice with the globalization of organizations, telecommuting, and employees working during different shifts and often in different time zones. Unlike centralized meetings of team members, virtual meetings are not limited by size.

Along with the special logistics and technology considerations of how the group will communicate during meetings (for example, audio, video, chat boards, and so on), an additional consideration for virtual meetings includes how to build trust among individuals. If possible, as the team is formed, try to hold one face-to-face meeting to speed the development of trust. If this isn't possible, then the team or meeting leader will need to use a variety of techniques to enhance the trust-building process, including

- Creating a shared message board that can be used as a welcome board. For example, invite each meeting participant to post a short introduction, his or her location, expertise and skills, as well as personal interests and hobbies.

POINTER

Identify one or two outcomes that are critical for deeming the meeting a "success." This ensures that the meeting content and participants are focused on achieving specific goals in the shortest period of time.

◆ Creating a small booklet that provides information about each team or meeting participant. If possible, include photographs so that each participant can visualize the people with whom he or she will be working.

Now that you've determined that a meeting is in fact the right approach, the next chapter covers the next step in the process—to create the meeting agenda and determine who needs to attend the meeting.

WORKSHEET 1.1
Meeting Planning Assessment

If you can answer "yes" to many of the following questions, then a meeting is probably in order.

❏ Can you state the purpose for the meeting?

❏ Is the meeting purpose worth the time and cost of taking the participants away from their jobs?

❏ Is a meeting going to be a more efficient and accurate way to convey information than sending an email or making some phone calls?

❏ Do you really want participants' input and not just a slate of agreements?

❏ Are you going to act on people's input?

❏ Do you have the information that you need to meet productively?

❏ Will you and your participants have enough time to prepare for the meeting?

❏ Are the participants going to be able to work together on the issue?

If in answering these questions, you have concluded that a meeting really is the best way to accomplish the objective, then your next step is to determine who to invite.

NOTES

_____
_____
_____
_____
_____
_____
_____
_____
_____
_____
_____
_____
_____
_____
_____
_____
_____
_____
_____
_____
_____
_____
_____
_____

Create the Agenda and Identify Participants

OVERVIEW

> Create a meeting agenda
>
> Estimate agenda timing
>
> Determine who should attend
>
> Choose the meeting time
>
> Define meeting roles
>
> Create the meeting invitation

The key to a successful meeting starts well before the meeting takes place—it begins with planning and creating the meeting agenda and identifying the right people who need to attend the meeting.

Create a Meeting Agenda

Some meeting leaders confuse the agenda with objectives. Objectives are topics or subjects to be accomplished (for example, to identify three solutions with the most impact on the current customer service issues). A meeting agenda lists the topics and the order in which they will be covered. When sequencing the meeting topics try to structure the topics logically, always keeping the purpose of the meeting in mind. When creating the agenda, consider these guidelines:

POINTER

As a best practice, send the agenda to participants along with the meeting invitation. This enables them to review the topics to be covered and to help them prepare in advance.

POINTER

Break the agenda topics into subtopics. Detailing the meeting agenda to a more granular level enables you to estimate the amount of time required for the meeting more precisely.

◆ Cover the topics in order of importance, with the most important topic first. Doing so takes advantage of early meeting energy and guarantees full coverage of the most important topics.

◆ Some experts recommend the reverse—that is, covering the least important topic first and building to the most important topic. This technique enables participants to warm up and get minor matters out of the way.

◆ If one topic naturally leads to another, a sequence of topics placed in a logical order often works best.

◆ Try to end the agenda on a positive note—something you expect will gain general approval from participants.

◆ Fill in activities planned to cover each topic. For example, the activities for one topic may be group discussion and debate, whereas the activities for the next topic may be stating an identified problem and brainstorming of solutions.

◆ Note how much time you expect each activity to take. Allow enough time for full participation by meeting attendees.

Estimate Agenda Timing

After creating an agenda that lists the flow of all topics and activities that you'll need to accomplish the session objectives, you need to assign realistic time frames for each activity. These estimates serve as a barometer for the pace of the meeting and allow all objectives to be met.

As a best practice, try to break the agenda topics into subtopics at enough of a detailed level for you to estimate the meeting timing as accurately as possible.

When creating the agenda, breaks should be slotted for every 60 to 90 minutes. As a guideline, it is usually better to schedule smaller and more frequent breaks—for example, two 10-minute breaks—than one longer break. Five-minute breaks are okay if you are really pushed to get things done on a tight schedule, but you should plan a minimum of 10 minutes for each break to allow enough time for participants to stretch their legs, check phone calls, and visit the restroom so they can return refreshed and ready to focus on the meeting objectives.

Table 2.1 provides a sample agenda, including a recommended level of detail, as well as time estimates and who is expected to lead each section of the agenda.

Finalizing the meeting agenda will not only help you to keep the meeting on track, but it will also be useful when you evaluate the success of the meeting and whether the defined goals have been accomplished.

POINTER

Avoid Friday afternoons when determining the time of the meeting. Participant energy may be low, and this time is often used to finish up items that are due before the weekend.

STEP **2**

TABLE 2.1

Sample Meeting Agenda

Time (min)	Topics and Subtopics	Lead by
20	Introductions	Mary
	Purpose of the Initiative	
	Team Roles and Responsibilities	
	Meeting Objective: • To identify three strategies to implement now to address the top customer service issues.	
10	Brainstorm Subsequent Meeting Ground Rules	Mary
90	Discuss current customer service issues and survey feedback	Tom
	Brainstorm causes and possible solutions	
	10-minute break	
	Prioritize causes based on the biggest impact to the customer	
45	Breakout groups to discuss implementation strategies	Bob and Sue
10	Break	
30	Group discussion on implementation strategies, impact, and costs	Mary
10	Break	
15	Determine the top three strategies to implement now • Use weighted decision table	Mary
15	Assign action items and responsibilities	Mary
	Meeting wrap up	

Determine Who Should Attend

In planning the agenda, the leader should determine who should attend the meeting for each agenda item. People's time is a valuable resource both in terms of what it costs and in terms of what else they can achieve in that time. For that reason, you need to ensure that the people asked to participate in the meeting are those most likely to contribute and help to achieve the desired business outcomes.

Once the meeting objectives have been determined, there are two basic criteria to determining who should be at a meeting:
1. those who can *benefit* enough for it to be worth their time
2. those who can *contribute* enough to justify their time.

Both of these criteria require subjective judgment. There is also a third criterion to be considered: those who want to be at the meeting.

Some people want to attend to satisfy their egos. Others want to be there to get firsthand knowledge of what happens in the meeting. In some cases, a strong negative attitude might develop if a particular individual is not invited to the meeting. So, at times it is important to invite participants just because they want to be there.

If the meeting's purpose is to discuss a controversial issue, make sure you invite an equal number of participants from both sides of the issue. And make sure that both sides of the issue are represented by people of equal status.

Be sure to consider the number of participants on your list. Is it a manageable group in view of the objectives you need to accomplish? If, for example, the only objective is to have participants hear about a new policy, you can achieve that objective with a large group. If, however,

POINTER

Assign roles to facilitation session participants such as notetaker, timekeeper, and parking lot attendant.

there is another objective such as brainstorming ways of applying the new policy for profit, a shorter list of participants will be more effective when conducting the brainstorming segment. Usually groups of no larger than 10 are best for decision-making and problem-solving sessions.

After identifying the participants, the next step involves determining what you need to know about each person to accomplish the meeting's stated objectives as well as identifying what each person's responsibilities for the meeting will be. For example, do you need

- to know in advance whether each participant has experience with the type of project to be discussed
- to be aware of what each person's expectations are concerning the initiative
- someone to provide specific background information
- someone else to come prepared with suggestions and ideas for discussion
- the participants to read a report and be able to discuss it intelligently?

Try to schedule a break every hour. It is better to schedule two 10-minute breaks rather than one 15- or 20-minute break for longer meetings.

You also have to determine if you need everyone to attend the entire meeting or only a part of it. To use people's time most effectively, perhaps structure the agenda so that people not needed for the entire meeting are listed first on the agenda so that they can participate and then leave the meeting when it is no longer relevant for them to continue to stay. When participants are only needed for one item, another option is for them to stand by until the group reaches that item on the agenda.

Know the Meeting Participants

In an ideal situation, you have all the information you need about the meeting participants before beginning a meeting. Usually, that is not the case—so meeting leaders need to ask, "What do I need to know about the meeting participants to accomplish the meeting objectives?" As a best practice, consider gathering

◆ the skill and background levels of the participants

◆ job context information, including whether the participants work alone or in groups; levels of activity and movement they are accustomed to; and where they are in their work cycle when they attend the facilitation session (for example, are they just ending the graveyard shift and showing up for the session exhausted?)

◆ the learning styles and preferences of participants and what they are or are not accustomed to

◆ the level of flexibility, openness to change, willingness to share opinions or try new ways of doing things

◆ the participants' attitudes toward the topic(s) to be discussed

◆ circumstances leading to their participation (is it mandatory or voluntary?).

Taking time to gather this information prior to the facilitation session will help arm you with the key information required to structure the meeting and to plan appropriately how many and what types of activities might be most effective to achieve outcomes.

If you do not have time prior to the facilitation session to identify this information about the participants, plan some contingency activities such as an opening or warm-up activity to gather this information at the start of the session.

Choose the Meeting Time

Choose the Meeting Time

Determining the time of the meeting is very important. First, consider when the meeting leader and presenters are available and how much time is needed to adequately prepare. Just as important is the availability of the participants. If the participants have a negative attitude toward the time, the leader will have a more difficult time accomplishing the objectives. Participants with negative attitudes are not very eager to understand information that is presented or to participate in problem solving.

The best way to select the right time is to ask meeting participants for their preference. The selection of the meeting time should include both the starting and concluding times. If the length of the meeting can be predicted and controlled, then the quitting time should be communicated to the participants in advance.

Define Meeting Roles

A key task to planning highly productive meetings includes defining the meeting roles and responsibilities. For example, the sponsor or planner of the meeting may or may not lead the meeting. For that reason it is important to define the role of who will lead the meeting discussions. This may be one or more people depending on the type of meeting, the topics of discussion, and the need for subject-matter experts to lead the discussions for topics in which they are most familiar.

POINTER

When determining the meeting time, try to keep the meeting as brief as possible. A meeting should never run longer than 90 minutes without a break.

Role of the Leader

Meeting leaders are ultimately responsible for the quality and effectiveness of the meeting achieving its defined goals. That includes everything from showing up on time, respecting the views of all participants, sharing opinions, managing facilitation and decision-making processes, clarifying views and opinions so that all participants can follow the dialogue, and helping the group come to consensus on decisions.

A strong understanding of how the meeting leader's role may change depending on the type of meeting is important, however. Keep in mind that the leader's role is ultimately to ensure the quality and effectiveness of the meeting in achieving the defined goals no matter what type of meeting is taking place.

Additional Meeting Roles

Productive meetings are conducted in an efficient, smooth manner and are documented for follow-up action. To accomplish this, meeting leaders may need the help of participants to function as time-keeper, facilitator, notetaker, and parking lot attendant. See the Meeting Roles pointer for details of each role. If the meeting is a recurring meeting, such as a project status report, then assign the roles to a different person each time. Whatever you ask of your participants, make sure that you give them a sufficient amount of time to prepare.

Create the Meeting Invitation

How many times have you been in a meeting and found that you have information relevant to the topic, but you weren't asked to bring it, nor asked to review it in advance?

Successful leaders provide appropriate notice to participants. Sometimes significant lead time is not available to send invitations—especially if the amount of time between the decision to have the meeting and the time of the meeting is slim. Although that is understandable, it isn't acceptable if the meeting leader

POINTER

Meeting Roles

Leaders enlist participants to perform these rolls:

- **Timekeeper**—Effective meetings start and end on time. To help make that happen, use a timekeeper. The timekeeper notes the amount of time allotted on the agenda for each activity and keeps track of the actual amount of time spent. If the group goes beyond the allotted time for an activity, the time-keeper interrupts (gently) and asks the group to make a decision: Should they continue the activity now or at a later meeting? If a discussion is particularly productive, moving other agenda items to another meeting can be worthwhile, but first gain agreement from participants.

- **Facilitator**—Facilitation is a highly desirable skill set that requires learning and practice. People often underestimate its importance and difficulty. During a meeting, the facilitator has two main jobs: 1) to draw out quiet participants and 2) to prevent other participants from dominating the discussion. To draw out quiet participants, consider
  - asking by name if the person has anything to contribute
  - recognizing when someone has made a contribution
  - asking a question and have everyone respond to it at one time.

A slightly sneaky way to keep someone from dominating the discussion is to assign that person the role of the facilitator. Other ways include interrupting gently and asking someone else for his or her opinions or reminding everyone of the time limits on agenda items.

◆ **Notetaker**—The notetaker serves as the official historian for the meeting. Depending on the structure of the meeting, he or she might take notes on a flipchart and periodically confirm with the group that points are recorded accurately. Alternatively, the notetaker may keep notes on a pad of paper or electronically, use an electronic whiteboard, and so on. No matter how notes are captured during the session, as a best practice, they should always be typed up and distributed to all participants after the meeting.

◆ **Parking Lot Attendant**—A parking lot attendant captures any ideas or topics that arise in the meeting but are not on the agenda. Parking lot attendants often capture this information on a flipchart or other designated place. These ideas may be more relevant to subsequent meetings or may have value that the group decides to visit at a later date in order to stick to the current meeting agenda. Capturing these items enables the participants to focus on the current topics and keeps the meeting moving forward. By designating a meeting participant for this role, the leader can indicate what items should go in the parking lot as they come up yet keep the meeting going. This way, the meeting leader is not burdened or distracted by having to capture this information while the meeting participants wait for it to be written down.

Role of the Leader

Depending on the type of meeting the role of the meeting leader often varies:

- **Informational meetings**—In this type of meeting, the role of the leader is to communicate information so that the group understands it. In these meetings, the leader might do all of the talking with little to no participation from the group. If the meeting does allow for group participation or a question-and-answer session, then the leader may do 90 percent of the talking.

- **Problem-solving meetings**—This kind of meeting requires an entirely different role by the leader. The leader must get attention and clarify objectives. Often the leader provides background information and subsequently participates 10–20 percent of the time, whereas the group dominates the discussion 80–90 percent of the time. The role of the leader is to get the group to participate and to control the participation to accomplish the objective. In this type of meeting leaders may also jump into various roles during the meeting, including presenter, stimulator, participant, and controller.

♦ **Facilitative meetings**—Groups, a basic work unit of organizations, are often tasked with providing different views on a topic or issue, solving problems, coordinating complex work processes, and so on. In facilitative meetings, the leader serves as the facilitator—a person who has no decision-making authority within a group but who guides the group to work more efficiently together, create synergy, generate new ideas, and gain consensus and agreement. In this type of meeting, the leader focuses on helping to improve a group's processes—meaning how the group works together, including how they talk to each other, identify and solve problems, make decisions, and handle conflict.

♦ **Instructional meetings or training sessions**—In this type of meeting, the leader serves as a teacher or instructor. The percentage of participation depends on the subject, the objectives, and the knowledge and experience of the group, as well as on the personal style of the leader. For example, if the leader is a subject matter expert in the content, and if the group has little knowledge, then the leader may spend 75–90 percent of the time lecturing or presenting. If the leader prefers discussion, case studies, games, and breakout activities, then the time the leader spends presenting may be evenly split or perhaps as much as 80 percent of the participation will come from the group.

neglects to send a meeting invitation and agenda in advance. Proper notice is necessary so that participants can plan to attend the meeting and do whatever preparation is necessary. Another benefit of providing advanced notice to participants is modeling the appropriate behavior that you expect of other meeting participants. Providing advance notice shows that you respect the participants' busy schedules and demonstrates that you are making every effort to ensure that everyone can attend.

When sending meeting invitations to participants consider these five main items, as shown in Figure 2.1, which should be included in every invitation:

- time (starting and ending times, unless it is a problem-solving meeting in which a quitting time is only suggested)
- place
- objectives
- preparation to be done by participants such as premeeting reading, research, or work assignments
- names of other participants.

Plan Effective Meetings: The Fundamentals

No matter what their purpose, all productive meetings share similar characteristics. Responsibility for these characteristics and conditions is shared by the meeting leader and participants. To help get your meeting session off to the right start, focus on these characteristics:

- All participants have a valid reason for being included in the meeting.
- All participants know the purpose of the meeting and arrive prepared to fulfill that purpose.
- The meeting is as brief as possible and sticks to the agenda.
- Objectives, or desired outcomes, are determined in advance and are achieved by the end of the meeting.

- All participants leave the meeting knowing what was accomplished and what is expected of them in the future.

Now that you've created the meeting agenda and identified the right participants who need to attend, the next step is to design the meeting detail by creating effective openings, transitions, ground rules, stories, anecdotes, and closing activities.

FIGURE 2.1
Meeting Invitation Example

Customer Service Issues Meeting

Date:	4/15/20XX

Start: 9:00   **End:** 12:00

Location: Room 3B

Meeting Purpose:
To identify three strategies to implement now to address the top customer service issues.

Proposed Agenda:
(can copy here or include as an attachment in an email)

Invited Attendees:

◆ Mary S. – Meeting Leader

◆ Tom G. – Customer Service

◆ Bob F. – Breakout Group A Facilitator

◆ Sue B. – Breakout Group B Facilitator

◆ Dave L. – Notetaker

◆ Jacki B. – Timekeeper

◆ Mark M.

◆ Jennifer M.

◆ Tora E.

Premeeting Work:

In advance of the meeting, please read the customer survey feedback report.

Bring to the Meeting:

Please bring a list of issues that you think are causing customer dissatisfaction.

Lay the Groundwork for Success

OVERVIEW

The opening

The parking lot

Transitions

Techniques for generating discussion to accomplish goals

Guided discussion

Debriefing sessions

To lay the groundwork, the next step in the process is to plan the content flow and to develop the meeting leader notes and materials.

Most successful meeting leaders create a detailed outline that lists all activities that will take place during the meeting. They select meeting activities that focus on achieving the stated objectives and prioritize them in terms of importance.

Every successful meeting outline often includes the following components:

◆ **An opening**—which may include icebreakers, reviewing the agenda, clarifying the purpose and objectives, establishing ground rules, and explaining the purpose of the parking lot.

◆ **The tasks to be completed**—which can be facilitated with guided discussions, questioning techniques, transitions, stories, action planning, debriefing sessions, and so on.

◆ **A closing**—which often summarizes the key points and confirms responsibilities for action items and next steps.

This step in the process explores all of the components to consider when developing a detailed meeting outline.

The Opening

How often have you attended a meeting that quickly fell flat after the housekeeping details were discussed? The key to an effective opening and a successful meeting is enthusiasm! Enthusiastic involvement is required to get participants to want to attend the meeting. Their initial attitude toward being there is critical. To build this initial enthusiasm, the meeting leader must convince each participant that there is a need for the meeting and the participant's attendance. Whether the meeting leader speaks with enthusiasm, passion, and excitement about the opportunity or does so in a monotone—all set the stage. The leader's opening words establish the tone, pace, energy level, and expectations for the rest of the meeting.

POINTER

The best way to get the participants to understand that meetings will start on time—is to, of course, start on time. That means as a meeting leader you need to arrive at the meeting room early to get set up, test any technology that will be used, and be prepared to start promptly at the appointed time.

Icebreakers

So what types of activities and techniques engage the audience right from the start and help to create interest and enthusiasm? Icebreakers include several types of activities such as

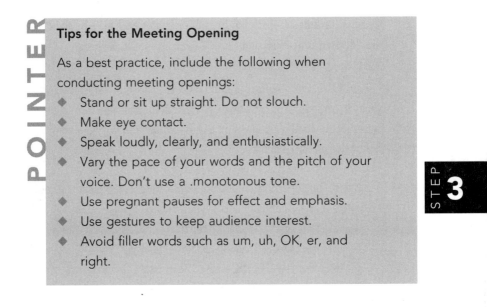

Tips for the Meeting Opening

As a best practice, include the following when conducting meeting openings:

- Stand or sit up straight. Do not slouch.
- Make eye contact.
- Speak loudly, clearly, and enthusiastically.
- Vary the pace of your words and the pitch of your voice. Don't use a .monotonous tone.
- Use pregnant pauses for effect and emphasis.
- Use gestures to keep audience interest.
- Avoid filler words such as um, uh, OK, er, and right.

openers, warm-up activities, and acquainters. These activities immediately get people involved, foster interaction, stimulate creative thinking, challenge basic assumptions, illustrate new concepts, and introduce specific material.

- **Openers and warm ups**—these icebreakers warm up a group by stimulating, challenging, and motivating the participants. They can be used to begin a session, start a discussion, prime the group after a break, or shift the topic focus.
- **Acquainters**—these icebreakers serve two functions: They establish nonthreatening introductory contacts, and they increase participants' familiarity with one another and usually are not tied to the meeting content directly.

For more information on icebreakers, see Step 7, which provides specific examples of icebreakers.

Openers

Openers differ from acquainters in that they introduce or tie into the topic of the meeting. They are intended to set the stage, avoid abrupt starts, and make participants comfortable. They may energize groups after coffee breaks or lunch and may be used to open subsequent meetings.

An effective opening is crucial to the start of any meeting because it bridges from whatever the participants were doing before the meeting to the purpose of the meeting, the agenda, and the tasks they need to achieve.

A meeting opening should not only help establish the credibility of the leader, but also accomplish three things:

- grab the participant's attention
- express the main goal of the meeting
- express the benefit and explain what the participants can expect to get out of the facilitation session.

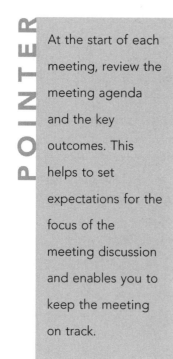

At the start of each meeting, review the meeting agenda and the key outcomes. This helps to set expectations for the focus of the meeting discussion and enables you to keep the meeting on track.

Openings should both explain the topic of the meeting and capture the audience's attention. Do not attempt the second without covering the first. Remember, if your attention-grabber does not tie into the topic, you will only confuse and distract the participants. Here are some best practices for openings:

- State the purpose or goal of the meeting. All participants will want to know why they are there and what is expected of them early in the process.
- Make the opening relevant to real-life experiences. This helps participants grasp the topic of the meeting by relating it to something they understand.

- Ask questions to stimulate thinking on the meeting topic. Besides stimulating the thought process, this technique helps participants focus on the topic. These might be rhetorical questions or a show of hands.
- Share a personal experience or anecdote that is universal. You will spark participants' interest if they have experienced something similar. Limit your "war" stories; too many can turn off interest.
- Give a unique demonstration. This works well with technical topics. You can then proceed from the introduction to explanations of the "why" and "how" of the demonstration.
- Use an interesting or famous quotation, or perhaps turn this quotation around just a bit to fit the topic. For example: "Ask not what work teams can do for you, but what you can do for your work team."

Establishing Ground Rules

Ground rules are behavioral expectations that leaders and participants have of each other to support the group's efforts. Developing ground rules can be an excellent opening activity. Depending on which activity will work best, you can:

- Present a list of proposed ground rules and facilitate an activity in which the participants react to and revise them.

POINTER

Use a parking lot to post any discussion items or questions that are not relevant to the meeting's focus but should be addressed either outside of the meeting or in a subsequent meeting. The parking lot is an effective tool to demonstrate that participants' questions and concerns are noted but also keep the meeting moving forward to accomplish the stated goals.

STEP **3**

◆ Facilitate an activity in which the participants propose their own ground rules and then come to consensus or vote on them.

The best way to get buy-in is to have the group define its own ground rules for the meeting. If you feel that the group has overlooked an area, such as confidentiality, that should be addressed, ask them to consider and decide how they would like to handle it.

When the group establishes and agrees on the ground rules, post them so that they are always visible. Quite often individuals will "self-police" other meeting participants when any ground rules are broken. Depending on the formality of the environment, there are many ways to gain commitment from participants, ranging from the participants simply committing to point it out verbally, to verbalizing a key word, and to throwing paper wads or Nerf balls at the offender.

It is best to display the ground rules every time the group meets. Don't shortchange this process! The up-front time spent is well worth it! Not only do ground rules help to keep discussions on track, but they also promote and maintain friendly group relations. To help you get started, consider using these ground rules:

◆ meetings begin and end on time
◆ all attendees must actively participate
◆ cell phones, PDAs, or any distracting items are turned off
◆ one person speaks at a time
◆ no side conversations are permitted
◆ respect others and their opinions, even if different from yours
◆ speak up if you have something to say
◆ what is said in this room is confidential and stays within the group
◆ the group needs to come to consensus when making decisions. If necessary, the group will vote to come to agreement.

The Parking Lot

A parking lot, another frequently used tool, is often a flipchart or other designated place to collect ideas or topics that arise but are off the agenda. These ideas may be more relevant to subsequent meetings or may have value that the group decides to visit at a later date so as to stick to the current meeting agenda.

Capturing these items in the parking lot enables the participants to focus on the current topics and keeps the meeting moving forward while acknowledging ideas or questions that need to be addressed at a later time. Parking lot items should be documented and revisited at the end of the session to determine if they should be addressed outside of or in subsequent meetings.

Transitions

Transitions help you move from topic to topic in a smooth, seamless manner. They are segues to the different parts of your meeting outline and are important in making the dialogue cohesive and understandable. For example, "Now that we have discussed the main customer service complaints outlined in the survey report, let's begin to work in groups and brainstorm what you think are the best solutions that can be implemented quickly and that will have the biggest impact in resolving these issues for our customer."

POINTER

Establishing meeting ground rules is a key task when leading a one-time or recurring set of meetings. The ground rules enable you to get buy-in from the participants regarding what is accepted behavior (for example, no cell phones, active participation required, do not discount someone's opinion or point of view, and so on). When the group establishes and agrees to the ground rules, post them so that they are always visible.

STEP **3**

Techniques for Generating Discussion to Accomplish Meeting Goals

After planning the meeting opening, the next step in developing the meeting outline is to plan the activities that will guide the group to achieving the desired outcomes. For example, an outcome might be for the group to create a list of 10 suggestions to assess the current morale of a particular department. As you are designing the meeting outline, select the most appropriate tool or technique to lead to the desired outcome.

Successful leaders leverage myriad facilitation techniques and master when to use a particular technique as much as how to use it. Some basic techniques include:

◆ **Listening**—If you expect the group members to actively participate, then you need to be sure to listen to what they are saying. After posing a question, pause and give them time to think and formulate their responses. When someone begins to respond, avoid assuming that you know what he or she is going to say. Nothing dampens a group's discussions faster than a leader who interrupts or jumps to hasty conclusions about a particular point—which may be incorrect. Pose a question, give the audience time to think, and then truly listen to participant input.

◆ **Questioning techniques**—Using various questioning techniques is probably the most common way to encourage participation from a group—and is a skill that serves business professionals both inside and outside of a meeting room. There are several types of questions, including open-ended, close-ended, hypothetical, and rhetorical. The ability to ask strong questions requires skill, practice, and planning.

◆ **Accepting different opinions and views**—If you are asking for ideas, comments, and thoughts on a topic, then be prepared for views that differ from yours. If you don't agree with something, be sure that you do not leave the audience with the impression that you agree or that the information is correct if it is not. If answers to questions aren't quite on target, then redirect the question and open it up to others by asking, "What do the rest of you think?"

◆ **Silence**—Silence is an effective meeting technique and one that novice leaders often struggle with the most. Pausing enables the group to process what you are saying and to form their own thoughts and opinions.

Some additional considerations that you might want to include when creating your detailed agenda and notes to lead the meeting are guided discussion, storytelling, humor, quotations, metaphors, and analogies.

Guided Discussion

Guided discussions are a type of structured exercise that enable meeting leaders to ask the group a series of planned questions designed to get them to wrestle with topics and issues at a deeper level. As they answer the questions, the facilitator summarizes their content and may also play devil's advocate to drive for deeper content or application, and guides the discussion to the next question.

Storytelling

Storytelling is an interesting, proven, and inexpensive way to prepare examples from your own experiences. Stories are often memorable, people like to hear them, and they tend to be a useful technique to capture an audience's attention and illustrate key points.

We all know presenters, facilitators, and meeting leaders who seem to have an innate ability to tell stories. They are able to pull out an appropriate tale, with a poignant message, just right for the situation or group at hand. The art of good storytelling is a learned skill that comes with practice. You can start a story to get discussions going and leave the rest of the story for later. Or, you can begin the story and then ask the group, "What do you think happened next?"

When thinking through story development, remember a good story has a beginning and an end. Consider the best point in time to begin your story, and develop an engaging start to draw in participants. Think about the pinnacle moments in the story, and how you can leverage them for maximum impact. And of course, your story should have a natural and clear ending. Practice telling the story a few times prior to the meeting.

Perhaps the most important characteristic of an effective storyteller is the ability to remain authentic—meaning, staying true to your own stories and maintaining the integrity of stories you select to retell. This means sharing truthful and relevant facts and detail.

Avoid "Winging It"

Winging it with examples and stories doesn't work. You can get off schedule in a big way. If you select a story to tell on the spot, you might be stealing your thunder for a later content point. You might get to the end and discover that the main point isn't really relevant to the content at hand. Some meeting leaders even get to the end of a spur-of-the-moment story and realize that not only does it not make a point, but also that the punch line is offensive. Think through your telling of examples and stories.

POINTER

Create an interesting meeting by including a variety of elements that will engage the participants and generate dialogue. These include icebreakers, questioning techniques, storytelling, anecdotes and metaphors, and so on.

Humor

Humor and laughter help improve, maintain, and enhance participant interest in a meeting. Camaraderie begins to develop when the leader and participants share a pun, story, or other common experience. Humor fosters a "team" atmosphere and promotes a positive experience.

Here are some tips for using humor, jokes, and funny stories during facilitation sessions:

- ◆ The humorous item must be relevant to the session topics and discussion at hand. Telling a story or joke just for fun takes the meeting off track.
- ◆ Avoid humor that might offend or alienate participants. Make sure your joke or story is clean. Perhaps this cautionary note seems obvious, but for some leaders, it isn't. Using even mild curse words is offensive to some participants and makes you look unprofessional. Don't think that if your audience swears, you can too. Part of your role as a meeting leader is to model professional behavior.
- ◆ Laugh at yourself, particularly when a story or pun flops. This puts the participants at ease and indicates that you are comfortable with the group and self-confident about your skills in leading meetings.

Quotations

Quotations from others that are strategically planned in the beginning, middle, or end of the meeting often have the effect of stimulating people's thinking. Before you use a quote, though, be sure of its authenticity—especially if you found it online—and its relevance to the subject matter. When you use a quote, always give attribution to the appropriate source.

Metaphors

Metaphors, as well as analogies and anecdotes, are thought-provoking forms of speech that open people's minds to think differently about a subject or issue. A metaphor is a figure of speech in which a word or phrase literally denoting one kind of object or idea is used in place of another to suggest a likeness or analogy between them.

One presenter at a career development seminar used the New York marathon as a metaphor for the effort involved in searching for a new job. As he painted a picture in the minds of his audience of the daunting task of running the marathon, he explained that conducting a job search was similar because those who are successful in completing the journey in the shortest time are always the ones who spend the most time preparing themselves.

Analogies

An analogy is a resemblance in some particulars between things otherwise unlike. Analogies, like metaphors, often help paint a picture in people's minds that help people to "see" concepts or ideas more clearly. One meeting leader, wanting to lay the foundation for introducing the agenda with regard to a new financial reporting system, used this analogy: "My understanding is that trying to reconcile the old monthly financial reports was like putting together a jigsaw puzzle only to find some of the pieces missing." Nodding their heads in agreement, the participants became eager, wanting to learn more about this new, less frustrating system and the project.

Debriefing Sessions

Once you have led the group through guided discussion after a structured exercise or activity, you will need to conduct a debriefing session. Debriefing sessions are designed to gather insights from the activity, summarize the main points, and help participants come to agreement.

Closing Activities

The end of a meeting is usually what participants remember most, so it is important to make the ending memorable. Take the time to plan the closing activity. The length of time required for this segment of the meeting depends on the length of the meeting itself. For example, a four-hour meeting may have a 15-minute closing activity, whereas a two-day session may require an hour for the close. A good closing should accomplish these things:

- **Review and summarize**—Take a few minutes to summarize and review what was covered during the meeting. Go over the agenda points and indicate what you covered, what was not covered, and any possible items for another meeting.
- **Discuss outstanding questions**—Allow at least five minutes of question time at the end of the meeting summary to ensure that everyone has the same perception of the meeting as you do and there are no points of confusion.
- **Gain agreements and commitments from participants**—End the session with the group agreeing on the content and outcomes of the meeting. In addition, each person should have made a commitment to further action. Make sure that each person is able to state what he or she is going to do and when. Plan to follow up at a later date.
- **Evaluate the session**—Periodically distribute an evaluation form to maintain and improve meeting quality.
- **End on time** (or better yet—a few minutes early!)—Show that you respect the participants' time and end the meeting when the agenda said it would end. If there are agenda points that did not get covered, then plan to have another meeting. If possible, end on a high note and always thank the group for their time and participation!

Worksheet 3.1 will help you to formulate your meeting outline and follow the planned meeting structure and activities to keep you on track to accomplish your objectives efficiently.

With the content flow and detailed leader notes crafted, the next step in the process is to identify the appropriate meeting room(s) needed to support your meeting and all of the planned activities.

WORKSHEET 3.1
Develop and Structure Your Meeting

This worksheet will help you get started in developing and structuring a successful meeting that provides value to your audience. Every item in your detailed agenda should be included to support the achievement of the meeting goals. If it does not—then it should not be part of your meeting plan.

Component	Tips	Meeting Outline and Flow
Meeting Objective	Decide if the meeting objective(s) can be accomplished in the time allotted for the meeting. If not, perhaps only list one or two objectives for the meeting and tackle the others during subsequent meetings.	**Objectives:** 1. 2. 3. 4. 5.
Openings should: 1. Grab the audience's attention. 2. Express the main point. 3. Express benefit and WIIFM.	Consider using jokes, humorous or relevant stories, anecdotes, icebreakers, brief exercises, imaginative visuals, provocative statements, unique demonstrations, or compelling questions.	**Opening:**
Transitions: Examples: "First, second . . . " "To begin, next" "On the other hand . . ." "To the contrary" "As a result . . . "	Create a transition for each agenda topic to segue and create a cohesive flow in an understandable manner.	**Transitions:** 1. 2. 3. 4. 5.

THE ULTIMATE IN CPLP™ TEST PREPARATION

ASTD LEARNING SYSTEM

Your self-paced, self-directed CPLP™ study guide with 10 complete volumes detailing the entire body of knowledge for the workplace learning and performance profession.

CHECK YOUR KNOWLEDGE! THE ASTD LEARNING SYSTEM COMPANION STUDY TOOL

Track your test prep progress with 650+ interactive questions to check knowledge, review content, uncover opportunities for improvement, and understand rationale behind answers.

ASTD LEARNING SYSTEM FLASHCARDS

For faster learning and longer retention—250 color-coded cards filled with 500 questions, definitions, and graphics to customize your study experience.

Order all three of the above CPLP™ test preparation resources in one comprehensive package and save.

10 volumes / CD-ROM / 250 Flashcards

Product Code: 180812

Member Price: $504 (reg $563.95)

List Price: $674 (reg $753.95)

Visit www.store.astd.org and search by product code 180812 to order.

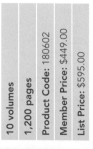

Meeting Topics	The meeting should have as many topics and subtopics as needed to accomplish the goals and objectives.
	
	Breaking down the meeting plan into subtopics enables you to plan the meeting at a more detailed level and to estimate the time required more accurately.
		Topics, Subtopics, and Activities to Engage Participants
		
		1.
		  ◆
		  ◆
		  ◆
		
		2.
		  ◆
		  ◆
		  ◆
		
		3.
		  ◆
		  ◆
		  ◆
		
		4.
		  ◆
		  ◆
		  ◆
		
		5.
		  ◆
		  ◆
		  ◆

Closing: **Examples:** Brief review Summary Next steps Action Items and responsibilities Final Q&A	The end of the meeting is usually what people remember most—so make it memorable. This should include a summary of what was accomplished, action items, and next steps.	**Closing:**

STEP 3

NOTES

_____

_____

_____

_____

_____

_____

_____

_____

_____

_____

_____

_____

_____

_____

_____

_____

_____

_____

_____

_____

_____

_____

_____

_____

Identify Appropriate Facilities

OVERVIEW

Large- versus small-group considerations

Best technology versus no technology

Room setup

Temperature

Lighting

Audiovisual setups

Many meeting leaders pick the most convenient place to hold a meeting. Frequently, this is a bad choice. Several factors should be considered in selecting the right place for your meeting:

- availability of the room at the time of the meeting
- large enough to comfortably accommodate the participants as well as any audiovisual aids
- appropriate furniture, including tables and chairs (the longer the meeting, the greater the need for comfortable chairs)
- adequate lighting and ventilation
- free from interruptions and distractions, including noise and telephones
- convenience for participants
- cost.

Sometimes several of these criteria are in conflict with each other. For example, it may be convenient for participants and also free of charge to hold a meeting on the organization's premises. However, the facilities may be too small or too close to the offices of participants, which could lead to distractions (mental and physical) as well as interruptions.

A meeting leader once had to conduct a series of instructional meetings for a group of state employees in the courtroom of a county courthouse. It was the only room that was large enough to accommodate all of the participants, but it perhaps wasn't the ideal setting because there were only benches and no tables on which to take notes. The leader of the meeting was also "trapped" at the judge's bench because it was the only place in the room where all participants could easily see the leader, so moving closer to the participants when they asked questions or to add interest by interacting with them was impossible.

Large- versus Small-Group Considerations

The selection of a meeting location is very important because the attitudes of participants are affected by the choice. Leaders have more difficulty accomplishing objectives if the room is too hot, the seats are too uncomfortable, the whirr of air vents makes it difficult to hear, and if there is a constant din of noise bustling outside the meeting room doors.

In planning and preparing the physical arrangement of the meeting space, the leader must consider the objectives as well as the number of participants who will attend. If it is an information-giving meeting with many participants, then theater style (without tables) may be the best physical arrangement. However, if there are five participants in a problem-solving meeting, the best room setup is to have people sit around a table so they can all see and hear each other.

If the meeting is for training and instructional purposes, several effective approaches are possible. In fact, the physical arrangement may be varied for a series of different instructional meetings to best accomplish the specific objectives of that meeting.

Best Technology versus No Technology

Depending on the meeting goals and objectives, the leader will also need to determine what technology, if any, is appropriate to support the meeting goals and objectives. For example, if the purpose of the meeting is to discuss the status of a project and to understand if the project tasks are on time, over or under budget, and if there are any expected issues, then all participants only need to be armed with a notepad and perhaps an updated copy of the project plan. For other types of meetings in which the leader is sharing information or providing instruction, presentation slides, an LCD projector, projection screen, flipcharts, and various types of handouts may be required.

Room Setup

The way the room is arranged is essential to the success of the meeting. To help in determining the most appropriate meeting room setup and technology considerations—such as when you are using audiovisuals—review the room setup matrix in Table 4.1.

Rounds

The term *rounds* connotes the shape of the table used—but in terms of table setup, the table shape might really be square or rectangular. In this configuration, the meeting leader and any audiovisual equipment are usually found at the front of the room. Although the number of people at each table will vary, table seating usually averages between four and 10 people, depending on the number of tables and the size of the group. Rounds work well for groups of at least 15 people, especially when you want them to work in small groups. This setup creates a friendly environment with flexibility to choose the best audiovisuals to support the meeting.

Setting up rounds requires a room large enough to allow ample space between the tables without chairs brushing up next to each other. The biggest challenge of using this setup is that some

TABLE 4.1
Room Setup Matrix

Style	When to Use	When Not to Use	Alternatives
Rounds	• Larger groups • Work in teams • Small-group interaction • When using audiovisuals	• Room too small • Group less than 15	• Classroom • Chevron
Classroom	• Any size group depending on room size • When using audiovisuals • When focus is on the presenter	• You want group interaction • Room dimensions are too long or wide	• Chevron • Rounds • U-shape
U-Shape	• Smaller group size • Open environment • When using audiovisuals	• Small room • Large group • Work in teams	• Classroom • Chevron • Conference
Chevron	• Large groups • For presenters who like to move • When using visuals	• When a warm, personal atmosphere is needed	• U-shape • Rounds • Classroom
Conference	• Small group • Group discussion • Formal and intimate	• Room to spread out • When using audiovisuals that require room • Presenter movement	• Classroom • U-shape

participants may need to crane their necks to see the leader or audiovisuals based on the position of their chairs.

Classroom Style

This is similar to traditional school classroom seating with rows of desks or tables and chairs all facing the facilitator, who is standing in front. This type of arrangement usually creates a formal tone with all eyes on the leader and does not allow for a great deal of movement or interaction among participants.

Most participants will be able to easily see both high- and low-tech visual aids, including flipcharts, whiteboards, and presentation software or slides. If the room is very long or very wide, however, some participants may feel like they are in the remote recesses of the room and may have difficulty seeing visuals. This setup is the least conducive to facilitating group discussions and interactivity.

U-Shaped Configuration

This room configuration is often popular for group and workshop-type settings in which all participants can see each other and the leader has plenty of room to walk around. This setup is particularly useful when you want to have groups of two or three people talk or work together.

This setup works best for groups of 12 to 24 people if the room is large enough. If the group is too big or too

POINTER

When planning and preparing the physical arrangement of the meeting space, consider the objectives as well as the number of participants who will attend, and select the most appropriate meeting room setup to support the planned activities such as working in groups or breakout activities requiring additional rooms.

small, then that defeats the purpose of this room setup. Be careful not to cram too many tables and chairs into a room that is too small. This will make it difficult for participants to walk around the outside of the table, and leave the room when needed.

Chevron

This arrangement combines the best features of the classroom and rounds arrangements. Like the classroom setup, rows of tables are placed angled and positioned behind each other. This placement forms the letter "V" with a main aisle in the middle. Like the rounds setup, it makes for easy pairing of groups already set at different tables.

This setup offers two main benefits. It can accommodate large groups and because the tables are angled, participants can easily maneuver and walk around the room. This setup also enables the leader to easily walk down the main aisle and to make a variety of visual aids visible to the group.

One disadvantage is that the participants in the back of the room, even with the tables angled, might have difficulty seeing some of the visuals if the group is large. This type of setup also does not create a very warm or intimate arrangement because most of the participants are looking at the backs of the people in front of them.

Conference Style

This style usually involves the group sitting in chairs around a large conference table. The leader can take a seat at the table, either at the head for a stronger presence or at any chair for a more informal effect. This type of arrangement works well for both formal and informal meetings if the group is relatively small, depending on the size of the room.

Keep in mind that some participants might be a bit confined if they cannot walk around the table. This setup is also not as conducive to group activities as rounds or other setups.

Temperature

Because room temperatures can vary wildly, ensure that participants and you will be comfortable. Prior to the meeting be sure that you find out how to control the room temperature. For example, can you adjust it yourself within the room or do you need to call someone within the building or at a remote location to request a temperature change? Here are some guidelines to consider:

◆ Set the thermostat for a comfortable level, depending on the season, size of the room, and number of participants.

◆ It's probably best if the room is cool at the start of the meeting because the room will heat up as more people join and audiovisual equipment throws off heat.

◆ Keep the room cooler if the participants are likely to wear business suits, which are often made of wool.

◆ For a daytime meeting in a room with windows, consider the effect of sunlight on the room temperature. Adjust the curtains or blinds—and perhaps the thermostat— accordingly.

POINTER

The selection of the meeting room is very important, and the venue will affect the attitudes of participants. Leaders have more difficulty accomplishing meeting objectives if participants have negative attitudes such as, "It's too crowded," "It's too noisy," "It's too hot," or "The chairs are too hard."

STEP 4

Lighting

Lighting is an important factor in creating a comfortable environment for the participants. Not only does lighting affect the mood of the participants (prime sleepy time after lunch), but it is also a key factor in how well the participants can see visual aids and their ability to take notes.

Just as you need to know how to adjust the room temperature, lighting is no different. Be sure that you know how to dim and change the lighting.

POINTER

When determining whether to hold a meeting on-site or off-site, keep in mind that off-site meetings usually mean additional costs in terms of the facility, equipment rentals, as well as travel expenses of participants. So, the investment in holding a meeting off-site can be quite substantial. As such, the meeting results should also be as substantial to make the investment worthwhile.

Audiovisual Setup

Chances are you'll be using at least one type of media to support the meeting. Although visuals can really enhance and clarify issues and ideas, they can also turn the meeting into a disaster if you haven't appropriately planned and specified what you need in the meeting room. Make sure you have accounted for the following prior to the meeting date when using visual aids:

- Verify that there are enough outlets to accommodate all audiovisual equipment needs. Know the location of each and arrange for any extension cords or power strips.

STEP 4

- Tape down or cover any cords or wires that might pose tripping or electrical hazards.
- Familiarize yourself with each piece of equipment before the meeting and "cue up" any visuals.
- Prepare a contingency plan if any equipment malfunctions, such as locating replacement bulbs, batteries, and so on.
- Identify the on-site audiovisual contact and how he/she can be reached should you need help.

POINTER

Identify the on-site contact in case there are technical or other issues with the meeting room that are different from what you specified. Confirm the procedures that you should follow if for some reason the designated contact cannot be reached the day of the meeting.

Food and Breaks

It's not unusual for continental breakfast items or snacks to be readily available in the meeting room or immediately outside the door. In fact, you might even be asked to conduct a meeting over lunch or dinner. Because food service can affect the meeting—if you have any say in the matter—consider the following:

- Get to know the people who are handling the food service, and be clear about your expectations regarding the kinds of food that will be served, and when, how, and where the food will be set up.
- Opt for lighter, nutritious fare such as fruit or pasta salads, and small sandwiches. Heavier food tends to make people drowsy, especially right after lunch or in late afternoon. Arrange for plenty of bottled water and juices as alternatives to sodas, as well as both decaffeinated and caffeinated coffee and tea.

POINTER

Confirm all of the peripherals that you will need to support the meeting and confirm whether you, other meeting participants, or the facility is providing them (for example, flipchart paper, flipchart easels, markers, LCD projectors, masking tape, power strips, and so on).

◆ If possible, ask for the food service to be set up in advance so that it does not interfere with the meeting. If this is not possible, arrange for the food to be set up outside the meeting room to minimize the noise and disturbance.

Now that the options for room setup and the specifics of the meeting environment have been detailed, use Checklist 4.1 to ensure that you have considered all the arrangements necessary to host a successful meeting.

With the room logistics out of the way, the next step in the process is to facilitate the meeting. We focus on how to hone your skills and facilitate with the meeting objectives in mind.

CHECKLIST 4.1
Meeting Room Setup

Use the following checklist when planning and setting up the meeting location so that the environment supports the accomplishment of the defined meeting objectives.

	Room Setup Considerations	Notes
❏	What size room do you need for the type of meeting and activities that you plan to take place?	
❏	Will everyone be able to see the meeting leader or speaker as well as any visual aids used (for example, flipcharts, whiteboards, projection screen, and so on)?	
❏	Is there enough room for all audiovisual equipment?	
❏	Is there enough room between tables and chairs for participants to easily navigate around the room without distracting or bumping others?	
❏	What type of meeting room configuration is best with regard to the setup of tables and chairs to accomplish the meeting objectives (for example, rounds, classroom, U-shaped, chevron, conference, or theater)?	
❏	Is smoking allowed? If so, should a non-smoking table be designated? If smoking is not allowed, how far do smokers need to go from the meeting room to access a smoking area?	
❏	Will breakout rooms be needed? If so, what types of equipment or supplies are required for those rooms (for example, flipcharts, markers, tape, and so on).	

STEP 4

(continued on next page)

Room Setup Considerations	Notes
❐ What arrangements need to be made during breaks or if the meeting runs over multiple days to ensure that the cleaning crews do not throw away meeting materials?	
❐ Can the air and temperature in the room easily be controlled, either centrally in the room or by another source?	
❐ Is there enough space on walls and panels to display charts?	
❐ Should name tents be included, especially for initial meetings, so that the leader can use names of participants and other attendees can become familiar with other group members?	
❐ What type of audiovisual equipment is needed? Do the walls contain enough electrical outlets? If computers are to be used, will antisurge electrical outlets be needed?	
❐ Is there any source of noise in the room (for example, street, alleyway, loading dock, building renovation, elevators, and so on)?	
❐ Are there any noisy sessions planned for adjacent rooms—especially if the meeting room has a dividing wall or partition that might not block noise?	
❐ Do the chairs have wheels that might permit them to be easily moved without noise? What is the comfort level of the chairs (a must for longer meetings!)?	
❐ Is there sufficient space for whiteboards and flipcharts?	

Room Setup Considerations	Notes
❏ Are there any technology considerations to include or purposely exclude—such as Ethernet connections to access organization servers or the Internet?	
❏ If there are any technology challenges or needs during the meeting, who is the on-site contact and how do you get hold of the contact?	

NOTES

_____

_____

_____

_____

_____

_____

_____

_____

_____

_____

_____

_____

_____

_____

_____

_____

_____

_____

_____

_____

_____

_____

Use a Reliable Process to Facilitate the Meeting

OVERVIEW

Step-by-step problem-solving method

Types of facilitation tools

Process tool application

Groups tasked with providing different views on a topic or issue, solving problems, coordinating complex work processes, or implementing change initiatives are often ineffective in getting decisions made and procedures in place.

STEP **5**

Enter the facilitative meeting. In these types of meetings, the meeting leader (or other skilled person) plays the role of a facilitator—that is, a person who has no decision-making authority within a group but who guides the group to work more efficiently together, create synergy, generate new ideas, and gain consensus and agreement.

The purpose of facilitation is to guide a group to an agreed-upon destination or outcome. As such, facilitators often point participants in the right direction, make suggestions, take steps to enhance the experience for the participants, and offer guidance—but do not do the work for group.

The purpose of facilitation is to guide a group to an agreed-upon destination or outcome. As such, facilitators often point participants in the right direction, make suggestions, take steps to enhance the experience for participants, and give guidance—but they do not do the work for the group.

Step-by-Step Problem-Solving Method

Groups are notoriously inefficient at solving problems and making decisions. This phenomenon is often due to the fact that groups and many business professionals are unfamiliar with a formal problem-solving process and the facilitative tools to help a group skillfully navigate this process.

Successful meeting leaders ensure that groups follow an organized procedure involving problem identification and solution generation no matter what goal is to be achieved. Regardless of the purpose of the meeting—for example, strategic planning, long-term planning, succession planning, or general problem solving—consider following the process method listed below.

Step 1: Identify the Desired State and Generate Ideas

Many groups, anxious to jump in and start making decisions, often shortchange this step in the process. Problem definition is critical to identifying the desired state and what success looks like when goals and objectives are achieved.

The synergy and differing views derived by working in groups is often greater than one individual working alone at his or her desk. However, each individual in the group brings his or her own views and ideas—so this step in the process can be a windfall in truly assessing and defining the problem if the facilitation process is given the appropriate time to cull this information from the group.

At this stage, the group should focus on being explicit about the language used in defining terms and what they mean to all individuals in the group. Participants should be pushed to provide specific descriptions and examples, as well as to question assumptions and perceptions.

Step 2: Define and Analyze the Problem

Sometimes the problems a group must address are not obvious to all participants. Groups rarely make decisions in an empirical vacuum—rather they must go through the due diligence of gathering the right information to help them make informed decisions. Intelligence involves gathering relevant data, both objective and subjective, that is pertinent to the decision the group must make.

Depending on the timeline of the project and time constraints to get decisions made, the facilitator or meeting leader may try to gather as much information as possible prior to convening a facilitative meeting. Several instruments enable meeting leaders and facilitators to efficiently gather information, including surveys, focus groups, group interviews, and so on. This information may come from internal or external sources such as customer or employee feedback, technical experts, and subject matter experts.

POINTER Groups are notoriously inefficient at solving problems and making decisions. This is often due to the fact that groups and many business professionals are unfamiliar with a formal problem-solving process and the facilitation tools to help a group skillfully navigate this process.

STEP **5**

Step 3: List Possible Solutions

Teams often jump to this step in the process. However, effective teams resist that temptation and move systematically through the process.

At this point, it's time to get all thinking caps on and generate multiple ideas and solutions. When promoting idea generation, successful meeting leaders and facilitators encourage groups to consider all possible options. This means stating the ground rules of not criticizing or discounting any ideas at this point in the process and not settling too quickly on any one option.

All individuals make decisions based on a set of criteria. For groups to succeed in their mission, everyone needs to understand the criteria and agree to weightings regarding the importance of each criterion in making a decision.

Perhaps a group is responsible for identifying at least five vendors with the capabilities to implement a new application in the organization. The mission of the group is to not only identify and create a list of five vendors but make a recommendation regarding which vendor should be awarded a contract. Then, the group defines a list of system requirements and weighs the "need to have" requirements more heavily than others. Summing the requirements scores might help the group to determine which vendor to recommend for the contract.

Step 4: Evaluate and Choose the Best Solution

This stage involves systematically evaluating each potentially viable option against the criteria and choosing the "best" options (that is, the ones that stack up best against the criteria). This is the appropriate point in the process for the group to become critical about the ideas generated.

During this final step in the process, successful meeting leaders and facilitators help the group to clarify discussions, summarize the results of evaluating and narrowing solutions, keep the group on track, and try to help the group reach consensus so that everyone "buys in" to the final decision.

In the vendor-selection example listed previously, perhaps the group determines that the vendor who meets most of the requirements is not the best option if the vendor cannot implement the new application within the given timeframe or if the vendor is twice as expensive as other vendors.

POINTER

General problem-solving and decision-making methods can be applied to any situation—meaning that the steps and tools used transcend most any type of facilitating meeting regardless of the specific session goal(s).

Types of Facilitation Tools

Effective team decision making depends on defining the problem. Simply stated, a problem is a discrepancy between what is and what should be. A problem should be stated in the form of a question; for example, "How can we reduce the number of defective widgets produced daily?" is better than "Develop a plan to reduce scrap material."

Depending on where the group is in the problem-solving and decision-making processes, facilitators use different tools to support and guide the group as well as the process. Table 5.1 lists categories of tools to facilitate idea generation, problem definition, problem analysis, and decision making.

When selecting the appropriate tool, facilitators need to consider:
- What process step is the group in?
- Are they trying to generate ideas, evaluate ideas, or come to agreement on the best solution?

TABLE 5.1
Facilitator Tools by Process Step

Purpose	Tools
Identifying Problems and Generating Ideas	◆ Brainstorming ◆ Sticky Note Brainstorming ◆ Round Robins ◆ Mind Mapping ◆ Fish Bone Diagramming
Defining and Analyzing Problems	◆ Mind Mapping ◆ Fish Bone Diagramming ◆ SWOT Analysis ◆ 5-Why Technique
Listing and Prioritizing Solutions	◆ Affinity Diagrams ◆ Nominal Group Technique ◆ Multivoting Technique ◆ Dots ◆ Matrixes and Decision Tables
Decision Making	◆ Pros and Cons Lists ◆ Voting

Brainstorming

In brainstorming, the idea is to come up with as many ideas as possible and then whittle them down to a couple that seem the most promising. Brainstorming promotes collaborative problem solving by getting the audience or small groups to focus on creating and expanding a list of possibilities.

The number of people who can participate has no limit, but presenters often break larger audiences into subgroups of four to five participants to create and expand a list of possible ideas or solutions. In brainstorming, record and recognize all ideas, no matter how outlandish. Postpone evaluation of ideas put forward until the next step in the process.

How to Use

Brainstorming is an excellent way to engage participants by posing a problem for which you want them to develop solutions or to generate a list of ideas related to a specific topic. When facilitating brainstorming, use these steps:

1. Assign a question or get the groups to agree on a central question related to the topic.
2. Each participant in the group needs to suggest at least one idea or solution to the question posed.
3. Have one person in each group capture all ideas generated—no matter how outlandish. Postpone evaluation of ideas put forward until the next step in the process.
4. Call time.
5. Depending on the purpose of the brainstorming session, have the groups either go back and select the top five ideas to develop further and refine—or—go back and generate ideas for each solution posed.
6. Have the groups review the completed list for clarity, duplication, and to make their final recommendations.

POINTER

Effective team decision making depends on correctly defining the problem. Depending on where the group is in the problem-solving and decision-making processes, facilitators use different tools to facilitate idea generation, problem definition, problem analysis, and decision making.

STEP 5

Sticky Note Brainstorming

One variation on traditional brainstorming includes using sticky notes to capture individually brainstormed ideas. The notes are then placed on a wall for everyone to see. This enables the participants to easily group the ideas by topic, category, feasibility, and so on.

How to Use

This activity is especially useful to get participants on their feet and moving around and makes it easy to group, prioritize, or whittle down ideas. Use these steps to implement this technique:

1. Provide participants with several large sticky notes (or index cards) and markers.
2. Direct the group to brainstorm and to legibly jot down one idea on each sticky note. If you are trying to gather contrasting information (for example, problems and solutions), perhaps have the participants document the information on different-colored notes or cards).
3. Instruct the group to place their sticky-note ideas on the wall (or within categories on a flipchart, and so on).
   - ◆ **Tip:** If you are trying to maintain anonymity, then collect the ideas and post them on the wall or flipchart yourself.
4. Ask the participants to come up and read all of the ideas.
5. Begin the group discussion and evaluation process to organize the ideas and begin whittling down the list.

Round Robins

In this technique, the facilitator gives each person an opportunity to state orally one idea pertinent to the question posed. Round robins encourage relatively equal participation among all group members.

How to Use

1. Pose a question to the group.
2. Give the group time to ponder the question and generate at least one idea. Stress that they may want to come up

with several ideas in case there are duplicates. The goal is to generate new ideas.

3. Call time.

4. Either ask for a volunteer or call on one person to state his or her idea, which is recorded publicly on a whiteboard or flipchart.

5. Go to the next group member and continue the process of asking for ideas and posting them. If any members have more than one idea, they need to wait until the next turn to express each idea.

6. Continue the round robin until all ideas have been stated.

Mind Mapping

This technique is also called idea mapping, clustering, webbing, and spidering. See Figure 5.1 for an example of mind mapping. It is a fast, fun method of free association that produces ideas. It helps members suspend judgment of ideas and can be used either individually or in a group.

How to Use

1. Instruct participants to write a word or phrase on a piece of paper that describes the problem.

2. Draw a circle around the problem statement.

3. For two minutes, write down all aspects of the problem.

4. Connect the related words with arrows or lines.

5. Look for three or four main themes or categories, and assign a geometric symbol (for example, a square, circle, triangle, diamond) to each category.

6. Discuss the findings.

Fish Bone Diagramming

Sometimes stating the problem and clarifying it in a brief discussion is sufficient. Often, however, this is not enough, and you need more formal techniques to help the group work with an understanding of the problem. One helpful technique is called a fish bone diagram—also known as an Ishakawa diagram or cause-and-effect diagram.

FIGURE 5.1
Mind Mapping

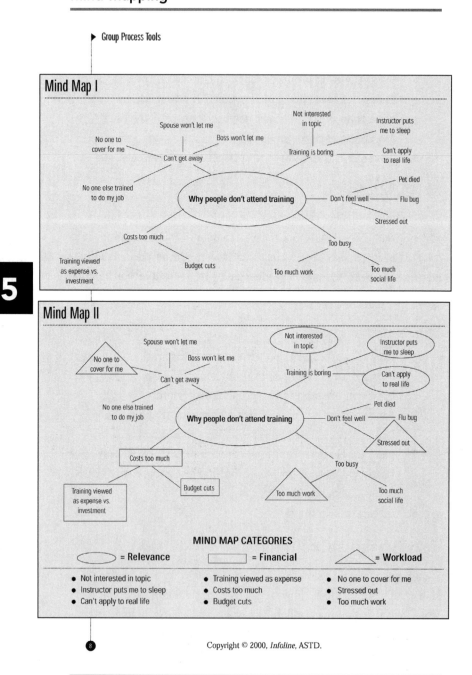

▶ Group Process Tools

Mind Map I

Spouse won't let me
Not interested in topic
Instructor puts me to sleep
No one to cover for me
Boss won't let me
Can't get away
Training is boring
Can't apply to real life
No one else trained to do my job
Pet died
Why people don't attend training
Don't feel well
Flu bug
Stressed out
Costs too much
Too busy
Training viewed as expense vs. investment
Budget cuts
Too much work
Too much social life

Mind Map II

Spouse won't let me
Not interested in topic
Instructor puts me to sleep
No one to cover for me
Boss won't let me
Can't get away
Training is boring
Can't apply to real life
No one else trained to do my job
Pet died
Why people don't attend training
Don't feel well
Flu bug
Stressed out
Costs too much
Too busy
Training viewed as expense vs. investment
Budget cuts
Too much work
Too much social life

MIND MAP CATEGORIES

⬭ = **Relevance**   ▭ = **Financial**   △ = **Workload**

- Not interested in topic
- Instructor puts me to sleep
- Can't apply to real life

- Training viewed as expense
- Costs too much
- Budget cuts

- No one to cover for me
- Stressed out
- Too much work

Copyright © 2000, *Infoline*, ASTD.

Fish bone diagrams emerged from the practice of quality assurance as a way of graphically identifying the factors affecting quality. In this context, facilitators use it as a way of identifying specifics that influence the desired state. For example, a group of executives looking at declining sales might incorrectly (or prematurely) conclude that the reason for the decline is inadequate marketing of the new products and services available. Rather than jumping to conclusions, the group could use a fish bone diagram to examine the range of factors that might be causing the problem. See Figure 5.2 for an example of a fish bone diagram.

How to Use

1. The group lists any and all factors related to the question or problem posed.
2. The group places the factors into categories. Examples of categories might be marketing, sales compensation, motivation, product design, customer satisfaction, and so on.
3. The group begins to fill in the diagram.
4. Each major branch (for example, marketing, customer satisfaction, and so forth) signifies one of the categories. The steps connected to the branch represent the more particular items from the original list. As the diagram grows, additional ideas emerge and the group adds them to the diagram.

What frequently happens is that one or two branches receives more attention than the others, and the group has an "a-ha" experience. Participants see the problem in a different light.

SWOT Analysis

A SWOT (Strengths, Weaknesses, Opportunities, Threats) analysis—also known as an internal and external environmental analysis—is used to determine strengths and weaknesses (internal) and opportunities and threats (external) of a particular situation. Another purpose of this analysis is to identify the contingencies that aid and

FIGURE 5.2

Fish Bone Diagram

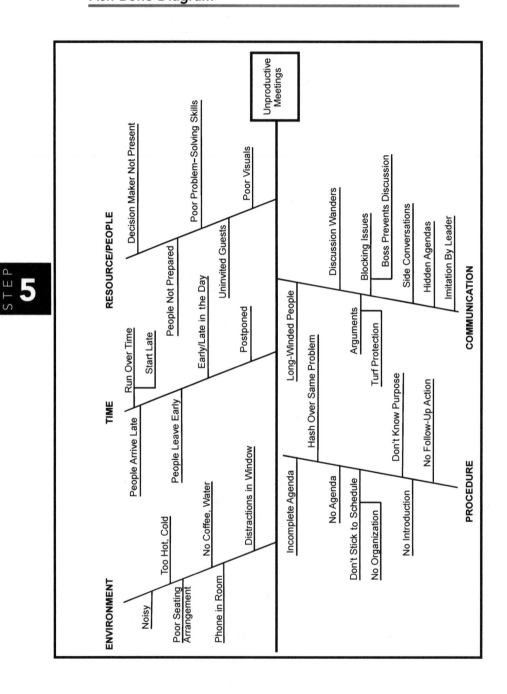

prevent an organization, department, group, or individuals from achieving a particular set of goals.

For example, a SWOT analysis considers

◆ **internal environmental factors**—including an organization's financial condition, managerial abilities and attitudes, facilities, staffing size and quality, competitive position, image, and structure.

◆ **external environmental factors**—including an organization's economic condition, legal and political realities, social and cultural values, the state of technology, the availability of resources, and the organization's competitive structure.

This technique is helpful as part of a background analysis for solving a problem.

How to Use

1. Create and display the chart below.

Strengths	Weaknesses
Opportunities	Threats

2. Use brainstorming or any idea-generation technique to have the group generate a list of ideas for each quadrant on the chart.
3. Using probing questions to get the group to delve into the details, define and explicitly explain their thoughts and rationale, and discuss the ideas at a deeper level.

4. Confirm with the group if they are ready to make a decision.
5. Use any of the techniques to gain consensus from the group.

5-Why Technique

The 5-why technique is a popular technique that tends to tell the story of causes and effects starting from back to front. It provides more depth than some other facilitation techniques and is useful with complex problems that stem from multiple or contributing causes.

How to Use

1. Write down the problem.
2. Ask the group to answer the question, "Why does this happen?"
3. Document the answers.
4. Turn each answer into the next why question (for example, "Why does this happen?").
5. Repeat for five iterations.

Keep track of relationships between cause statements and the next level of why.

Affinity and Interrelationship Diagrams

Affinity diagrams (also referred to as affinity maps or groups) gather a large number of ideas, organize these ideas into logical groupings based on the natural relationships among items, and define groups of items. A follow-up to the affinity diagram is the interrelationship diagram, which charts cause-and-effect relationships among the groupings. They are best used when issues seem too complex and relationships among facts seem confusing, when thoughts or facts are ambiguous or in chaos, or when the group needs to discover the major themes contained in a great number of ideas. See Figure 5.3 for an example of an affinity diagram.

FIGURE 5.3

Affinity Diagram

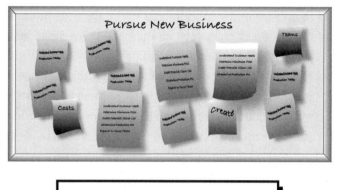

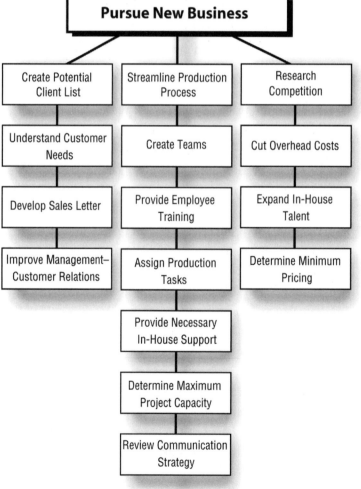

Pursue New Business

- Create Potential Client List
  - Understand Customer Needs
  - Develop Sales Letter
  - Improve Management–Customer Relations

- Streamline Production Process
  - Create Teams
  - Provide Employee Training
  - Assign Production Tasks
  - Provide Necessary In-House Support
  - Determine Maximum Project Capacity
  - Review Communication Strategy

- Research Competition
  - Cut Overhead Costs
  - Expand In-House Talent
  - Determine Minimum Pricing

STEP 5

How to Use

1. Phrase the issue to be considered. It should be broad, neu-tral, clearly stated, and well understood by the group.

2. Generate or record ideas. Working silently, each individual records his or her ideas in response to the issue or ques-tion on sticky notes (one idea per note). The group mem-bers hold all ideas until the next step.

3. Place notes on the designated surface. Without discussion, team members move to a specially prepared wall (covered with flipchart or butcher paper) or other flat surface and place the completed notes on the prepared surface. At this point, the notes are placed randomly on the surface.

4. Sort ideas into related groups. When all of the notes are placed on the surface, the group members, working in si-lence and moving quickly, use their "gut reactions" to move notes into related groups. Individuals can move any note anywhere on the surface. Disputes or disagreements about placement of notes are resolved silently. After a de-termined interval, the group is allowed to discuss their notes and finalize the groupings.

5. Create the category title. When all ideas are located in a category of related ideas, the group identifies the one idea or note that captures the essence of all the ideas on that group. This category title is written on the surface and lines are drawn to enclose all ideas related to that title.

6. Next, the group looks for interrelationships among the cat-egories. The group examines the categories to explore rela-tionships. The step in the process involves looking at each category and comparing it to other categories—asking the questions, "What is the relationship between these two? Which category causes or influences the rest?" If a relation-ship exists between two categories, the group draws a line that links the categories and notes the direction of the cause-and-effect relationship with an arrow.

7. Identify the key drivers. The last step in the interrelation-ship diagram involves identifying the categories that are

the primary drivers or influencers. For each category, total up the number of outgoing and incoming arrows and write the totals next to each category. The categories with the greatest influence—the primary drivers or causes—are those with the most outgoing arrows. Those with the most incoming arrows tend to be the results or effects of other forces on the page and therefore are not a high-leverage choice for effecting change in the outcomes. The purpose of this activity is to focus on the factors that have the greatest influence on the issue.

The outcomes of affinity and interrelationship diagrams are large groups of ideas categorized into related clusters of ideas, each with a clear title, and with the relationships clearly drawn. Furthermore, the key drivers or influencers are identified as a first step in developing a high-leverage strategy for causing lasting change in the system.

Multivoting, or Nominal Group Technique

Multivoting or nominal group technique is a structured method a team can use to brainstorm a wide range of responses to an issue, clarify each of the responses, and rank the responses from most to least important. Facilitators often use this technique with a team of representative stakeholders to minimize the impact of team dynamics in generating, evaluating, and ranking or selecting interventions.

How to Use

1. Agree on and write on a flipchart the issue facing the team. Post it so all can see it. Ensure that everyone understands the issue.
2. Ask each team member to develop a written list of ideas or suggestions. This is done individually, privately, and silently. Note that team members should record all their ideas, rejecting none.

3. After list making is completed, ask each participant—in a round-robin fashion—to offer one idea from his or her list. As each person responds, record the idea on a flipchart and number each item. Individuals may skip ideas already offered by someone else. Continue in rounds until the team has offered all its ideas.

4. After all ideas are recorded, lead the group in clarifying, linking, discussing, or eliminating ideas. Make notations on the flipchart to help improve understanding of each issue. The group should be aware that it is not necessary to agree that an issue is important; agreement is only needed on the meaning of the issue. The goal of this step is to reduce the list to a single roster of distinct, well-defined ideas.

5. Participants review the list and select their top five priority items. Each member notes on paper ballots the number of the item and a word or phrase that describes the item (one item per ballot). Then each team member rank orders the ballots from 5 (most important) to 1 (least important).

6. The team gives its ballots to the facilitator who records the numbers (5 through 1) from the ballots on the flipchart pages next to the item receiving a vote.

7. Total the points for each item. The item that receives the most points is ranked most important by the entire group.

The outcome of multivoting or Nominal Group Technique is a rank-ordered list of causes or solutions—each clearly defined and understood by group members.

Dots

This is a simple and time-efficient method for voting on ideas or solutions. It ensures that all members are actively involved, and it presents a visual representation of areas of consensus.

How to Use

1. List all of the previously generated ideas on a flipchart or large sheets of paper.
2. Give each participant an allotment of self-adhesive, colored dots.
3. Instruct participants to vote for ideas by placing a colored dot next to each idea. Dots can be allocated in any manner. For example, if each person is given 10 dots, all of the dots may be placed next to one idea, or three dots may be placed next to one idea and seven dots placed next to another.
4. Tally the votes. The ideas receiving the greatest number of votes are selected for further analysis or implementation.

Matrixes or Weighted Decision Tables

This method helps evaluate solutions against predetermined criteria. A major advantage of this method is that it recognizes the relative importance of each criterion.

How to Use

1. List the alternatives.
2. Brainstorm the decision criteria.
3. Evaluate the decision criteria and determine the importance of each.
4. Construct a matrix table (see Table 5.2 for an example).
5. List the criteria across the top and the potential solutions down the left-hand side of the matrix.
6. Using a scale of one to seven, with one being low importance and seven being high importance, ask the group to assign a value to each criterion.
7. Using the same rating scale, ask the team to rate each idea against each criterion. Record the rating in the upper portion of the diagonal line.

TABLE 5.2

Sample Matrix: Site Selection

CRITERION	Availability of Parking	Proximity to Public Transportation	Rental Fee	Capacity to Accommodate a Large Group	TOTAL
Criterion Rating	5	5	7	3	
Site A	4 / 20	1 / 5	3 / 21	7 / 21	67
Site B	5 / 25	6 / 30	3 / 21	5 / 15	91
Site C	3 / 15	5 / 25	2 / 14	6 / 18	70

Source: Barbara Darraugh, "Group Process Tools," *Infoline* No. 259407. Alexandria, VA: ASTD Press, 1997, pp. 9–10.

8. Multiply the rating for each idea by the weight given to each criterion, and write the product in the lower portion of the diagonal line.

9. Add the products for each idea and write the sum in the total score column.

10. The idea with the highest total score is the group's choice.

Pros and Cons Lists

Facilitators often use pros and cons lists to help groups evaluate solutions and to determine the best option or combination of options. The technique enables the group to look at all aspects of a solution before deciding whether or not to implement it.

How to Use

1. Create and display the chart on p. 83.

Pros	Cons

2. Brainstorm to have the group generate a list of pros and cons for a particular solution.
3. Instruct the group to evaluate the list and to comment on whether they are in favor of or against the solution. Try to get the group to delve into the details and discuss at a deeper level.
4. Confirm that the group is ready to make a decision.
5. Use the solution that the group agrees to.

Voting

Voting is a commonly used decision-making method. Although it helps the group to arrive at a quick resolution, it results in winners and losers. There are several types of voting in which each person has one vote, including

◆ **Simple Majority**—The decision is made when more than half of the group chooses the same solution.

◆ **Super Majority**—The decision is made when two-thirds of the group agrees to the same solution.

Process Tool Application

Now that we've outlined various general problem-solving processes that can be applied to any situation, let's look at how these same processes and the facilitation tools apply to strategic planning, as outlined in Table 5.3. Although we are using a strategic-planning meeting in this scenario, the processes and tools truly transcend most any type of facilitative meeting regardless of the specific session goal(s). Strategic planning allows organizations to make fundamental decisions that guide them to a developed vision of the future. Notice that although the strategic-planning steps may have specific names associated with them, each step falls within a step in the general problem-solving process.

TABLE 5.3
Applying the Facilitation Process and Tools

Process Step	Strategic Planning Step	Sample Tools
Identifying Problems and Generating Ideas	Defining the organization's mission and vision	• Brainstorming • Round Robins
Defining and Analyzing Problems	Researching the current state of the organization Establishing the target or future state and how success will be measured	• Mind Mapping • SWOT Analysis • 5-Why Technique
Listing and Prioritizing Solutions	Exploring and generating solutions to accomplish the goal	• Affinity Diagrams • Nominal Group Technique • Multivoting Technique • Dots • Matrixes and Decision Tables
Decision Making	Deciding on the solution	• Pros and Cons Lists • Voting

Use Worksheet 5.1 to determine the best techniques to use to get meeting participants engaged and involved so you can best accomplish your meeting goals.

With the core pieces of the meeting planned, the next step in the process involves preparing for the meeting, finalizing materials and handouts, and anticipating the unexpected.

WORKSHEET 5.1
Facilitation Planning

Use this worksheet to plan and select the most appropriate technique(s) to accomplish the meeting goals using facilitative techniques to engage participants and get them involved in the process! Review the techniques, definitions, and examples and add your own notes on how you plan to implement these during the meeting.

Technique	Definition and Example	How to Implement
❏ Listing	◆ Creating a list of items ◆ "Identify the three steps in which the process breaks down most often."	
❏ Grouping	◆ Categorizing information ◆ "For the list of customer complaints, what 2–3 categories do these fall in?"	
❏ Brainstorming	◆ Generating ideas ◆ "What types of changes can we make to improve the experience for our customers when they call in with questions or complaints?"	
❏ Prioritizing	◆ Identifying the items of greatest importance. ◆ "Of all the customer complaints on the list, which five should be given the highest priority to address?"	

(continued on next page)

Technique	Definition and Example	How to Implement
❐ Question and Answer	◆ Facilitating discussions, idea generation, and enabling participants to clarify information where the facilitator or other participants respond to questions, concerns, or issues. ◆ "What questions or concerns do you have about ?"	
❐ Small Group or Breakout Group Work	◆ Identifying problems, facilitating discussion, and generating ideas in a smaller, more intimate setting to create a climate of sharing. ◆ "Let's break into two smaller groups. I'd like group A to focus on how to change the business processes to improve customer service—and I'd like group B to focus on how to improve the morale of the customer service representatives."	

STEP **5**

Build a Game Plan for Success

OVERVIEW

► Prepare for the meeting

► Become familiar with the meeting flow and topics

► Finalize and organize your materials

► Be ready to answer questions

► Know the audience

Now that you have set the date for the meeting, sent the invitation to all required participants, and crafted the detailed agenda, most of the logistics needed to initiate the meeting are completed. The next step to conducting a successful meeting is preparing for the meeting day and polishing the final outline, timing, and meeting notes.

STEP 6

There are three keys to an effective meeting: preparation, presentation techniques, and audiovisual aids. Although the last of these is not essential in all meetings, it is highly desired in most meetings.

Several tips and techniques help you prepare for the meeting. This step of the process offers an opportunity to polish all content, to rethink structure, and to rehearse materials and presentation dynamics.

Good preparation by the meeting leader or speaker is essential because practicing builds confidence and helps to commit the flow and key points of the meeting to memory.

So how much time is appropriate for preparing and practicing before the meeting day? The amount of time required to adequately prepare varies based on the leader's experience, knowledge of the subject, and knowledge of the meeting participants. Knowing the material, transitions, and key points are a direct result of the time spent practicing and preparing. Because the time spent practicing is usually proportional to the level of relaxation you experience the day of the meeting—when you feel comfortable enough with the agenda, topic, and all meeting materials, then you've adequately prepared.

POINTER

The time required for you to adequately practice and prepare will vary depending on the type of meeting, your comfort level with the subject, who the audience is, and what presentation or facilitation method you are most comfortable with.

Remember, good meeting leaders demonstrate several key qualities during presentations:

◆ respect for self and for listeners
◆ honesty
◆ objectivity
◆ sense of humor
◆ adequate preparation
◆ balanced confidence and modesty
◆ verbal, vocal, and physical communication skills
◆ appropriate appearance.

When practicing and rehearsing to lead the meeting, focus on how and where each of these qualities will most likely occur during the presentation.

Prepare for the Meeting: Tips and Techniques

A key to preparing is to rehearse what you are going to say during the opening of the meeting. Memorize the first few paragraphs. Memorizing the opening comments and introductions usually reduces your stress level and gets the meeting started with the right focus.

Some meeting leaders write out every word they plan to say on note cards. Others take the opposite approach and think that they can "wing it" without notes because they "know" the subject. If you do not use any notes, though, a momentary lapse in concentration could throw the meeting into chaos because you have nothing to help you get back on track.

When polishing meeting notes, keep in mind that examples help participants to understand the concepts or topics presented or discussed. To capture participants' interest from the start consider

- varying the meeting's content and delivery
- using positive body language
- drawing parallels using what is already familiar to the participants
- sharing new and novel information
- discussing conflict, comparisons, and contrasts
- using concrete words and examples
- adding humor
- involving participants.

In addition to using examples that are relevant to participants' jobs, goals, needs, and interests, you can involve audience members by

- asking rhetorical, nonaccusatory questions
- calling for a show of hands
- directing the participants to look at something in the meeting room
- engaging them with questioning techniques and soliciting their opinions or feedback

- assigning participants to groups or teams to work in subgroups
- using brainstorming or other facilitative techniques.

Become Familiar with the Meeting Flow and Topics

The first 90 seconds of a meeting's opening are the most important because that's when the tone is set for the rest of the meeting. That's why great meeting leaders and speakers often visualize or memorize the first 90 seconds of the opening. Once again, it's all about being prepared. When you start strong, the participants become energized and engaged.

Once you know what you're going to say, consider some of these suggestions for that first 90 seconds:
- look like you're confident even if your knees are shaking
- acknowledge your audience, smile (if appropriate), and start talking
- exhibit an outward appearance that says to your audience that there isn't any other place you'd rather be
- begin by painting a mental picture with your words and actions for the audience right from the start
- focus, be positive, show enthusiasm, and speak confidently.

When creating and organizing your notes to lead the meeting, write out the key points in their entirety. Think about the organization of the topics and subtopics and rearrange slightly for clarity, if needed. If after rehearsing several times, you still struggle with the appropriate setup or transition to move from one topic to the next, write a "T" or "transition" on the meeting notes with a few key words to help you remember the key point to set up what's coming next on the meeting agenda.

Finalize and Organize Your Materials

If the meeting includes audiovisuals, then be sure to incorporate them when practicing. Work on smoothly transitioning between the meeting content and the audiovisual aids by

- referring to specific page numbers in handouts
- noting when to display the next slide in your notes
- identifying when to advance a slide for all of the animation or special elements to appear (for example, a red circle appearing over a specific section of a form or numbers on a spreadsheet to orient listeners to what you are referring to).

If you feel unsure or uncomfortable with the meeting flow and content, then you may want to rely heavily on a detailed outline of the meeting plan as a crutch to help you along the way. So what's a good way to organize these meeting notes?

One strategy includes typing a detailed outline or writing notes on numbered note cards. Be sure that you have a spare copy of the outline or note cards—just in case a pitcher of water spills and turns the ink into an illegible blot! If you're worried about forgetting the opening, transitions, or the conclusion, then jot down key words as quick reminders of the points or exact words to use. After adequately practicing and rehearsing, you'll probably be able to condense your typed notes or the number of note cards further.

Nothing helps to overcome nervousness better than knowing the material. To accomplish this goal, consider using some of these techniques to practice before a presentation:

POINTER

Use symbols in the margin of the notes as quick reminders. For example, a smiley face might remind you to smile and make eye contact. Drawing a clock or snail, or writing the word SLOW might remind you to slow your pace in a particular section.

- **Practice in front of a mirror**—Some people find this technique helpful, but it may subtly reinforce the notion that you're talking to and for yourself rather than the meeting participants.
- **Use a tape recorder**—This tool can be a good way to check your voice and diction.
- **Use a video camera**—This tool gives you an opportunity to observe your body language as well as hear yourself; however, like a tape recorder a video camera may discourage some people when they review their skills because they do not like the sound of their voice or their appearance.
- **Practice the speech aloud**—Practice pronouncing difficult words (or eliminate them), test your pace, and time the meeting delivery to verify the time allotted.

Do Your Homework and Be Ready to Answer All Questions

Questions during a meeting have two purposes: 1) to clarify information that is unclear to the participants, and 2) to engage meeting participants and facilitate communication.

Although some meeting leaders invite questions throughout the meeting, other types of meetings may be structured to hold all questions until a formal question-and-answer session at the end of the meeting. Use these best practices to maintain control and effectively manage any questions during the meeting or formal question-and-answer sessions:

- Anticipate questions the audience is likely to ask. Plan short, to-the-point answers.
- Invite questions by saying something like, "Let's get started. Now, what questions do you have? To give as many people as possible a chance to speak, please limit your question to one minute."
- Arrange for someone you know to ask the lead-off question. Hearing someone else from the group speak first

gives other participants time to think and provides psychological permission to take the floor. Admit that you know the questioner. Say, "I see my friend Sue's hand first. Yes, Sue?"

◆ Call on participants in different areas of the meeting room. If audience members might be categorized by gender, age, or ethic group, don't exclude that group. Also give each person you call on "equal time" up to the established limit.

◆ Listen with a neutral expression. Make eye contact with the question-asker, but avoid smiling, frowning, or nodding "yes" or "no." If you say, "That's a good question" to some people, those who do not win this praise may be disappointed. If you praise every question, you'll sound insincere.

◆ Stop long-winded question-askers. Break eye contact. Hold up your hand to indicate "stop." Say, "Let me respond to that." Say it twice if necessary. If a questioner still continues, handle this person like a heckler. (See Step 9 for tips on handling difficult participants.)

◆ Divide multipart questions. Answer the parts separately.

◆ Don't challenge question-askers with "Why do you ask?" If a question seems vague or rambling, say "Could you restate that?" If after the restatement you still don't get the point, use a phrase from the restatement to construct a question that you are prepared to answer.

STEP 6

Know the Audience and Have a Plan for Difficult Participants

Maintaining control of a meeting is much tougher when a participant behaves rudely or inappropriately. An additional consideration when preparing for a meeting includes anticipating some disruptive behaviors and how you plan to effectively

POINTER

Don't worry too much about overrehearsing; you'll know when it's time to stop.

deal with them. Please see Step 9 for more detailed coverage of this challenge faced by meeting leaders. Listed below are some of the behaviors you may encounter as a meeting leader and suggested methods for dealing with them:

- **Hair splitter**—Acknowledge the participant's point, then reiterate the meeting objectives and time constraints.
- **Nonstop talker**—Tactfully interrupt the participant; summarize the points made and call on someone else.
- **Chatterer**—Tell the chatterer that you didn't hear his or her comments and ask him or her to repeat them.
- **Know-it-all**—Recognize the participant's ability and ask him or her the most challenging questions.
- **Point repeater**—Reassure the participant that you heard and recorded his or her point, and ask if he or she has an additional point to make.
- **Angry participant**—Acknowledge the participant's anger and offer to help sort out these feelings.
- **Automatic doubter**—Reassure the participant that the group will carefully evaluate all ideas later.
- **Interrupter**—Interrupt the interrupting participant; ask that person to hold comments for a while until all of the information has been presented to the group and reassure him or her that questions and opinions will be solicited from the group.
- **Interpreter**—Ask the participant to let everyone speak for him- or herself.
- **Frequent head shaker**—Acknowledge the participant's body language and ask that person to explain why he or she disagrees with the point made. If the head shaking gets out of hand or is accompanied by eye-rolling or other distracting movements, ask the participant to stop the disruptive activity either during the session or privately during a break.
- **Doodler (or other displays of disinterest)**—At the break, ask the participant why he or she isn't participating. The person may be preoccupied with a pressing

concern or may simply be bored. If he or she is bored, find out why so you can work next time at making the meeting more engaging.

Now that you have reviewed the tips and techniques needed to prepare for the day of the meeting, use Worksheet 6.1 to identify your strengths and weaknesses. This tool will help take your effectiveness as a leader to the next level.

This step focused on one of the key ingredients needed when planning an effective meeting—preparation. The next step in the process includes tips and techniques to engage participants and to maintain their interest throughout the meeting.

POINTER

If the meeting is primarily informational and you have to communicate a lot of facts in a short period of time, announce that you'd like to hold all questions until a certain point in the presentation and that you'll be taking questions for 20 minutes (or whatever time is allotted). This will help you to say everything you need to communicate but still allow participants time to ask their burning questions.

STEP 6

WORKSHEET 6.1
Developing Your Skills

To become an effective meeting leader, work on honing your skills by strengthening your major weaknesses. Successful meeting leaders and facilitators continually develop themselves by reading; attending seminars or workshops; taking on challenging job assignments; coaching; and so on. Use this worksheet to continue to develop your skills in creating and leading productive meetings.

Instructions:
1. Describe one strength you want to hone and one weakness you want to overcome.
2. Identify the method for development and required resources.
3. Establish a timeline for your development activities.
4. Determine the required feedback so that you can gauge the extent of your improvement.

Describe One Strength

Method for Development	Resources	Timeline	Feedback

Describe One Weakness

Method for Development	Resources	Timeline	Feedback

NOTES

_____

_____

_____

_____

_____

_____

_____

_____

_____

_____

_____

_____

_____

_____

_____

_____

_____

_____

_____

_____

_____

_____

_____

Prepare for the Meeting

► Icebreakers

► Questioning techniques

► Effective visual aids and data

► Contingency plans

How often have you attended a meeting in which participants are asked to introduce themselves, after which come the housekeeping details, followed by a slow uninspired tempo for the rest of the meeting? Every meeting has enormous potential to be great. So what do meeting leaders do differently to create high-energy, engaging meetings versus those that fall flat? They consciously and diligently focus on techniques that add interactivity and excitement, build energy and momentum, and create interesting dialogue. These meeting leaders focus heavily on this step in the process because they know that once you lose an audience's attention, it is extremely difficult to gain it back! Consider gaining participant interest early and engaging them by

- ◆ using strategies to involve participants
- ◆ leveraging effective visual aids
- ◆ planning for when the meeting gets off track or when something goes wrong.

One strategy for getting participants involved includes sprinkling icebreakers, energizers, and questioning techniques throughout the meeting.

Although most people practice a presentation or prepare for a meeting by focusing on the verbal delivery, remember to practice the nonverbal aspects as well. Practice eye contact (look away from notes and direct your attention to different points around the room), hand gestures, voice inflection, and your body language in general.

Icebreakers

Every successful meeting outline begins with an opening—which often includes icebreakers. Icebreakers are tools used to foster interaction, stimulate group thinking, challenge basic assumptions, illustrate new concepts, and introduce specific material. These tools help to break the ice in kickoff or other types of meetings in which participants are meeting each other for the first time. They also increase participant energy levels at key points in the meeting or after a break. Although there are hundreds of different icebreakers, let's look at a few examples.

Name Bingo

This icebreaker is particularly helpful for kickoff meetings or when forming new groups and is often used so participants can learn names and facts about each other. Even if participants know each other, this activity can help them to become reacquainted after a period of separation or to find out little-known facts about participants.

Directions

Name Bingo can be modified to increase self-disclosure. Besides names, participants can be asked to obtain and record one fact about each person they meet on the Bingo form (see Figure 7.1 for Bingo forms).

◆ Use a 3 x 3 portion of a Bingo form if the group includes fewer than 10 people.

FIGURE 7.1

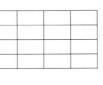

3 x 3 Form   **4 x 4 Form**   **5 x 5 Form**

◆ Use a 4 x 4 form for groups between 10 and 16.

◆ Use a 5 x 5 form for groups of 17 or more.

1. Hand out the Name Bingo forms.

2. Direct participants to mill around the room to meet other participants.

3. Each time a participant exchanges names with someone, he or she writes the name of the new person anywhere on the form (and perhaps writes down the one thing they learned about that person).

4. After 10 minutes, call time and direct participants to put a circle in any unused box.

5. Pass a hat around the group, one participant at a time. Each participant picks a name out of the hat. Everyone places an X on the Bingo form box for the name of the person drawn from the hat.

◆ As his or her name is picked, a participant introduces him or herself and shares a fun fact or bit of information about his or her interest in the meeting, being part of the team, or any other facts as appropriate.

   ◆ Any player obtaining all Xs in a row (horizontally, diagonally, vertically), yells "Bingo!" (Eventually, everyone will get Bingo several times.)

Because humor is a basic communication tool, it can be of immeasurable value in an icebreaker. Humor is a right-brain, creative activity that helps presenters to emphasize or reinforce the key and supporting points of a presentation. Humor provides a completely different perspective as an icebreaker. It can help relax the audience in tension-producing situations and can make a marginally interesting activity or subject more interesting, even exciting.

Two Truths and a Lie

This icebreaker is also useful when groups are forming but can also be used as an energizer at any point during a meeting when the group needs a pick-me-up. This tool is also helpful to use throughout different points of a particularly long meeting to refresh and invigorate participants with a mini mental break.

Directions

Ask participants to take a few minutes and jot down two truths (perhaps little-known facts about themselves) and one lie. At the opening of the meeting, ask for volunteers to share their three items and have the rest of the participants guess which one is the lie. This activity can be used for any size group. If the group has quite a few participants and the meeting will be fairly long, perhaps begin the meeting with half of the participants sharing their information, with the remainder of the group sharing theirs after returning from breaks or lunch. Don't be surprised if meeting participants remind you to go through more truths and lies as this activity creates a lot of enthusiasm!

Storytelling

Storytelling is an interesting, proven, and inexpensive way to communicate memorable messages. People like to hear stories, and in business, as well as other settings, storytelling works as a useful technique to

- capture a group's attention
- establish rapport
- build credibility
- build cohesion.

We all know presenters and leaders who seem to have an innate ability to tell stories. They are able to pull out an appropriate tale, with a poignant message, that is just right for the situation or audience at hand. So how can you harness this art of storytelling? Begin by reflecting on your past experiences, understanding the meanings inherent in them, and using those stories deliberately to send key messages in a variety of contexts and audiences.

Good storytellers have good stories because they listen for them and recognize when they are in one. Great stories might come from your own personal and professional experiences or the experiences of your colleagues or from within the organization.

Questioning Techniques

Using various questioning techniques is probably the most common way to encourage participation in a group—and is a skill that serves business professionals both inside and outside of a meeting room. There are several types of questions, including open ended, close ended, hypothetical, and rhetorical. The ability to ask strong questions requires skill, practice, and planning.

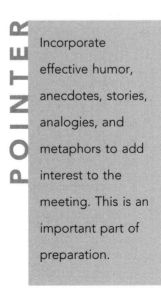

POINTER

Incorporate effective humor, anecdotes, stories, analogies, and metaphors to add interest to the meeting. This is an important part of preparation.

Open-Ended Questions

Open-ended questions usually require participants to respond using more than one

Try to anticipate difficult or other types of questions that are likely to be asked. Allocate time for the group to ask these questions and allow sufficient time for discussion and answers. The participants aren't likely to be angry if the meeting ends a few minutes early!

word—thereby expressing their thoughts, ideas, feelings, and opinions. For example, "Based on what we've discussed so far, how do you think this new process will affect your job?"

Asking an open-ended question is an excellent way of getting the participants involved in the meeting, increases the energy level of the session, and generates group synergy. Open-ended questions often start with

- ◆ "Tell me about . . . "
- ◆ "Why . . . "
- ◆ "What do you think about . . . "
- ◆ "How . . . "

Questions that start this way usually help the participants to expound on their answers, revealing information that can be helpful in discussion.

Close-Ended Questions

Close-ended questions are sometimes preferable to open-ended ones in certain situations. Close-ended questions are excellent for getting at specific facts and information. For example, "How many of you had a chance to read the information sent with today's meeting agenda?" You aren't interested at this point on if they agree with or are excited about the change or not, you only need to know the percentage of the group that has some baseline understanding of the topic to be discussed.

Close-ended questions often begin with

- ◆ "Who . . . ?"
- ◆ "Where . . . "

- "When . . . "
- "Did you . . . "

Hypothetical Questions

Hypothetical questions are great to get people thinking freely in situations in which many answers may be valid. They often start with "What if . . . ?"

For example, "What if we could implement a new process regarding _____ that would reduce the amount of time you spend on that task by 50 percent every day?" or "Where do you think this process will affect your workflow the most each day?"

Hypothetical questions are excellent discussion starters because they allow the participants to internalize a situation; think through any issues, problems, or solutions; and then actively discuss the impact of the issue at hand and their ideas on the issue. One warning—because hypothetical discussions are so effective at getting the audience to open up and join in the discussion, as a facilitator you may need to rein things in a bit to meet the agenda time constraints.

Rhetorical Questions

STEP **7**

Rhetorical questions—although really not questions at all—are used primarily to get the group thinking when you don't really expect them to answer the question aloud. These types of questions are used primarily for effect and to create excitement or interest in the topics and discussions to come.

For example, "We've all heard about the new process change and I know that change is sometimes difficult. But what if I told you that this new process has been proven to reduce workflow downtime by 50 percent?"

Effective Visual Aids and Data

POINTER

Be sure to proofread all visuals for accuracy, spelling, grammar, and content.

As the saying goes, a picture is worth a thousand words. Enter the value of visual aids. Whether you use visual aids to show what something looks like, or you choose text or other visuals to show how to do something, to clarify relationships, or to show how something is organized, four rules apply:

- make it big
- keep it simple
- make it clear
- keep it consistent.

Experienced presenters know that selecting the right way to communicate and deliver information is as important as what you say. That's where text, such as metaphors, analogies, and anecdotes, not only engage audiences but help you convey information more clearly.

When you need to discuss numbers and data to communicate relationships and trends, graphs or tables help your audience to visually see the information organized in a specific way to clearly communicate the trend or relationship that you are describing. The following guidelines should be considered when creating visual aids for meetings.

Text

For text visuals, use an easy-to-read serif (for example, Bookman, Palatino, Times) or sans serif (for example, Helvetica, Avant Garde) typeface. A mix of upper and lower case letters is easiest to read—don't use all caps or script. Keep graphic visuals uncluttered—don't be afraid of white space. Heavy grid lines, excessive tick marks, and other superfluous information will confuse your audience. Use only the data that you need to get your message across.

Tables and Graphs

To help participants in a meeting understand data or statistical information, consider organizing data or information in a table. Graphs are also an effective way to present data, show trends, and demonstrate relationships. However, some graphs are more effective at accomplishing these goals than others. In general,

- **Bar graphs**—show relationships between two or more variables at one time or at several points in time. Improve readability of a bar graph by making the bars wider than the spaces between them. As a general guideline, the audience should be able to read and understand the graph in less than 30 seconds.

- **Line graphs**—show a progression of changes over time. Be sure to label axes, data lines, and data points clearly. Be careful not to exaggerate the data points by changing the scale (for example, 0–100 or 1–50) or gridlines in the background to make something look more significant than it really is. Tick marks often clutter a graph—so use them sparingly and only if they add clarity for the audience. Gridlines or other graph elements that do not add clarity should be omitted.

- **Pie charts**—show the relationships among the parts of a unit at a given moment. Include only essential information

POINTER

When displaying text on slides, remember the guideline of six lines per slide and no more than six words per line. Text that is flush left with ragged-right justification is easiest on the eyes. For emphasis, use color, boldface, or larger type—make sure to use it consistently and sparingly.

STEP **7**

in pie charts and avoid having more than six wedges of the pie. Smaller pie slices can always be lumped into an "other" category.

Contingency Plans

Now that you've incorporated strategies to involve participants and created effective visual aids, the last step in the preparation process includes planning for when things go wrong. At times, as a meeting leader you may need to play the role of a neutral participant to smooth disagreements and calm flared tempers among participants. At other times, you will need to move the group along to accomplish the meeting goals and objectives. As part of your preparation process, be prepared to take charge and reframe discussions. You will also need to have strategies in mind in case you need to keep discussions on track.

Reframing

Successful facilitators use reframing as a technique to encourage participants to understand one another's point of view. Rephrasing any judgmental or blaming comments in another way and posing them back to the group helps to neutralize potentially charged comments and focus on the issues. This technique helps group members to hear each other in a neutral language so that they can continue to move forward with discussions and thereby accomplish their objectives.

Keeping Groups on Track

Being on track in a meeting means that the group is progressing with the agenda and working toward accomplishing the agreed-upon goal(s). That doesn't mean that the group needs to strictly follow the agenda minute by minute. As a meeting leader, at times you'll want to allow the group enough latitude for creative discussions, brainstorming activities, and healthy disagreements as long as they are helping to achieve the meeting goals. When trying to determine whether to let a discussion continue or to redirect the group in another direction, consider these guidelines:

POINTER

Learn as much as you can about the audience and backgrounds of the participants prior to the start of the meeting. Anticipate any multicultural or other types of considerations to create a meeting climate that fosters communication and sharing of ideas among all individuals.

- ◆ Review the agenda and determine if the time constraints allow for more discussion time.
- ◆ Review the ground rules regarding discussions that aren't relevant to the agenda and achieving the session objectives and determine if the topic should be tabled until a later time.
- ◆ Assess why the group has gone off track. Confirm that the participants are clear about the meeting goals.
- ◆ Point out the agenda and remind the participants of what needs to be accomplished and help them to understand the time requirements.

STEP 7

A good presentation requires self-confidence and enthusiasm. This chapter reviewed some tools and techniques to engage participants (and build your self-confidence) when preparing for a meeting. Enthusiasm comes from being convinced that the meeting content will be of value and benefit to the participants. Use Worksheet 7.1 to help formulate your strategy for opening the meeting, which will set the tone for your success in leading an interesting and effective session.

With the planning and preparation work out of the way—it's show time! The next step in the process focuses on how to conduct an effective meeting from start to finish.

WORKSHEET 7.1
Opening Meetings

The opening of a meeting sets the stage of what's to come. It greatly influences whether participants sit up and pay attention or check out and multitask. Use this list of ideas for opening a meeting to select your appropriate opening and plan how to customize it to support the meeting content and needs.

	Opening Idea	How to Customize for the Meeting
❐	**Jokes**—some meeting leaders like to lighten the mood by telling a joke. A joke can work if people find you funny and if you don't cross the line between good taste and bad. A general rule for jokes is if you have a question whether it would be appropriate to tell it, then don't.	
❐	**Humorous or relevant stories or anecdotes**—a story or anecdote can work well as an opening remark, but both require practice because few people are natural storytellers.	
❐	**An icebreaker or brief exercise**—an icebreaker is a brief exercise that often serves as a means for audience members to introduce themselves and to get to know each other. An icebreaker can be an effective way of starting your presentation provided that it's appropriate for the audience you are presenting to and you have enough time to do it.	
❐	**A question**—you can ask either a rhetorical question ("How would you like to learn how to become more credible in order to influence your organization in achieving its strategic goals?"), or you can ask a real question ("How many people find they have at least a little influence in their organization?"). In the former, you are not looking for a response, and in the latter you may simply call for a show of hands.	

(continued on next page)

Opening Idea	How to Customize for the Meeting
☐ **The successful [blank]**—after initial introductions, break into small groups. Ask the groups two questions: ◆ "Who/what was the most successful [blank] you've ever known?" ◆ "Why?" The meeting leader fills in the blank based on the meeting topic. The point of the opening is to have the groups build a model for the level of performance or behavior that is covered in the meeting.	
☐ **What's your problem?**—this opening activity is designed to prime a group for problem solving and to help raise awareness of an existing problem. Provide participants with an index card and ask them to divide it into three sections: ◆ My problem is . . . ◆ Barriers to doing it are . . . ◆ I am good at solving problems that . . . Have participants hold the cards in front of them while the meeting leader debriefs by leading a discussion on the identified problems and asking: ◆ How big (really) are these problems? ◆ How can barriers be overcome? ◆ Who would be a good resource for your problem?	

Opening Idea	How to Customize for the Meeting
☐ **Converting a tough audience**—this opening is for those occasions when you are dealing with touchy audiences—those who are required to attend the meeting and may not appreciate what the meeting can do for them. ◆ Ask participants to rate their personal productivity on a scale of 1–10, with 10 being perfect. ◆ Then ask them: "What is keeping you from being at a higher number?" Allow them several minutes to think this through. Most will identify several items. ◆ Finally, ask them "What is it costing you to stay at the lower number?" Allow them a few minutes to reflect. As they answer the question, arms typically unfold and ears perk up as the meeting leader explains how the meeting will address those specific issues. This process takes 15–20 minutes but can turn a tough audience into a receptive one.	

STEP 7

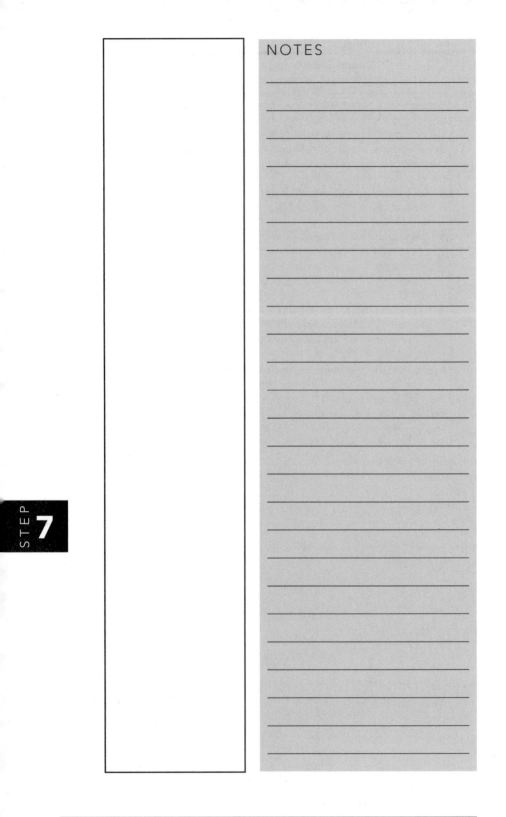

Conduct the Meeting

Regardless of the type of meeting, the leader must be in control if the meeting is going to be productive. Having control means you keep the pace moving so that objectives are accomplished in minimum time with satisfied participants. The best way to control a meeting is to prevent it from getting out of hand by clearly defining the meeting goals, starting and ending on time, establishing and enforcing ground rules, and using a parking lot. Aside from diligently managing those and other logistics, effective speakers and meeting leaders must demonstrate exceptional verbal and nonverbal communication skills—or participants will mentally check out and view the meeting as a waste of time.

STEP 8

Prepare the Room

Allow enough time before the participants arrive to get yourself and the room set up. As a best practice, consider the following:

- Check the seating arrangements.
  Are the chairs and tables the way
  you want them?
- Adjust the lighting.
- Check the audiovisual and computer equipment you plan to use.
  Be sure you know how to operate
  the equipment and that it's working properly.
- Arrange visual aids, such as
  flipcharts for documenting the
  meeting, brainstorming, or other
  activities so that everyone can
  see them.
- Check that you have allotted
  enough time on the agenda to
  cover all topics, have enough
  handouts (for example, the
  agenda, a list of meeting objectives, organizational flowcharts,
  and so on) for everyone, and that
  you have all materials needed for
  all planned activities, and so on.
- Display meeting objectives and
  the agenda. If plan to have the
  participants define the session objectives and goals, post either
  blank flipcharts to facilitate the
  activity or post defined objectives
  for them to react to and refine.

POINTER

At the start of the meeting, clarify the purpose of the meeting, the objectives and expected outcomes, and the time allotted to accomplish these items. Set the group's expectations early so that you (and other participants) can help manage the meeting in order to achieve these goals!

Begin and End on Time

A productive meeting always starts on time. Period. As a meeting leader, do not stop and restart the meeting for participants who arrive late. The participants arriving on time recognize that you are

ready for them and that you don't intend to waste their time. This recognition helps to set the climate for a productive meeting and lets everyone know that you will start meetings promptly as scheduled—so all participants will need to be on time as well. The most effective meeting leaders always display enthusiasm at the start of the meeting and throughout the session. Enthusiasm, optimism, and energy are contagious, so be energetic and upbeat from the start and maintain your enthusiasm throughout the meeting. When starting the meeting, ensure that everyone knows each other, introduce any participants who are new to the group, and consider structured icebreakers for the initial kick-off meeting or facilitation session to help group members introduce themselves and learn more about the other participants.

As a best practice, always review the meeting objectives and the agenda. You may want to also appoint participants to keep track of time and to record meeting notes. As the meeting is nearing a close, be sure to end on time (or better yet—a few minutes early!) to show that you respect their time. If there are agenda points that did not get covered, then plan to have another meeting. If possible, end on a high note and always thank the group for their time and participation.

Establish and Enforce Ground Rules

Ground rules are behavioral expectations that meeting leaders and participants have of each other. Developing ground rules can be an excellent opening activity. Depending on your assessment of which activity will work best, you can

STEP 8

- ◆ Present a list of proposed ground rules and facilitate an activity in which the participants react to and revise them.
- ◆ Facilitate an activity in which the participants propose their own ground rules and then come to consensus or vote on them.

The best way to get buy-in is to have the group define its own ground rules for the meeting. If you feel that the group has overlooked an area that should be addressed such as confidentiality, ask them to consider and decide how they would like to handle it.

When the group establishes and agrees to the ground rules, post them so that they are always visible for the current and any subsequent meetings.

Use a Parking Lot

One tool used by successful meeting leaders is the parking lot. This tool establishes a designated place to collect ideas or topics that arise but are off the agenda. These ideas may be more relevant to subsequent meetings or may have value that the group decides to visit at a later date. Documenting items in the parking lot enables the group to keep moving forward while avoiding tangents that may sidetrack the meeting progress. Parking lot items should be documented and revisited at the end of the session.

Communicate Effectively: Verbal and Nonverbal Skills

Everything that goes on in a meeting involves both verbal and nonverbal communication. Successful meeting leaders communicate effectively with groups using both verbal and nonverbal techniques and encourage this same behavior from participants. Review the best practices and "dos" for modeling verbal and nonverbal communication skills that get results:

- ◆ Maintain eye contact and exaggerate or animate facial expressions to show the group that you are enthused about leading the meeting. So how much eye contact is appropriate? As a general rule, spend five or six seconds of eye contact at least once with each member of the group, making sure that you look at everyone when facilitating. Eye contact is also an opportunity for a meeting leader or speaker to get a feel for how the group is reacting to the meeting, discussions, and other participants.

◆ Pause to add more emphasis in just the right parts of any meeting. This enables a key point to sink in and "silence" is often an effective technique to use to gauge audience reaction and to receive their feedback or ideas.

◆ Voice inflection is a key asset to capturing a group's attention and holding their interest. In any meeting, how you say something is just as important as what you are saying. Vary the tone, pitch, and volume of your voice so that you are not monotonous, lulling the participants into a slumber. Depending on the acoustics in the room, perhaps repeat comments or questions from meeting participants to ensure that all group members can hear and follow the dialog.

◆ Provide anecdotes or examples that are authentic and real for the audience. Although this is an important part of preparation, many times you will need to add these on the fly when conducting the meeting.

◆ Watch out and erase your use of filler words! These words creep into your speech to fill silence while you are thinking or transitioning to a new thought—for example, uhs, ums, ers, ahs, okay, right, and you know. Filler words are one of the fastest ways to annoy a group and even turn their focus to jotting down tick marks every time you use a filler word.

◆ Avoid distracting mannerisms with regard to body language— meaning how you look and move.

POINTER

Observe the group for nonverbal signals. This may indicate a lack of understanding (furrowed brow). Look for quiet individuals who appear as if they may have something to contribute but are hesitant to do so.

STEP **8**

Your body language can enhance or undermine your skills when leading a meeting. Based on different studies, it is usually accepted that between 7 and 10 percent of the effectiveness of a meeting comes from the words used. Because the remaining 90 percent of meeting effectiveness is attributed to nonverbal communication, speakers and meeting leaders need to be cognizant of their body language (and that of the group as well!), gestures, eye contact, and facial expressions to enhance communication and sharing of ideas.

◆ Above all, demonstrate enthusiasm and passion about the topic and the opportunity to facilitate. Your enthusiasm is contagious and often generates interest and positive feelings from the group.

Respect Multicultural Communication

Breakdowns in communication happen all of the time—both in and outside of meetings. So imagine the additional challenges presented when cultural aspects of language also affect communication within a meeting. Think about what takes place in meetings in which all participants' primary language is English. If participants in the meeting are from various parts of the country, some of them may have heavy regional dialects that even native English-speakers have difficulty understanding at times.

Depending on the part of the country, the rate of speech may vary widely as well. For example, the average speech rate in the mid-Atlantic states is 120–140 words per minute. In some metropolitan areas, for example, New York City, it may be even faster and considerably slower in southern states. Although it isn't ultimately the rate of speech that matters, the rate of speech does affect the ability of other meeting participants to clearly understand what is being communicated.

So why do people talk so fast? Often it is because others do this, and they want to quickly get in all of their key points before they are cut off or the meeting progresses to another topic.

In some cultures, speaking quickly is a sign of professional competence. Although language is important to facilitating communication in meetings—nonverbal communication is equally as important. For example, nonverbal cues such as eye contact, physical distance between participants, position of the seat where a participant sits in the room or around the table, as well as touching all mean different things in different cultures—and hence, may also be a barrier to communication.

So what can meeting leaders do to help facilitate clear communication when meeting participants' primary language is not English? Consider the following:

♦ Know your audience. The cardinal rule of any meeting preparation is always to identify the audience and perhaps to develop a profile of the audience. By understanding who will be attending the meetings and their backgrounds, you can plan ahead to accommodate the various cultures and backgrounds represented by all meeting participants. During this process, if you identify participants who may have some language barriers, perhaps reach out to them in advance and encourage them to

   ♦ Provide as many relevant documents possible in advance of the meeting so that they have time to review and formulate ideas and you can ensure that they understand the goals and premise of the meeting.
   ♦ Let them know that in many English-speaking cultures, silence is often a signal that someone understands the conversation at hand. Encourage them to ask questions if they do not understand what is being said during the meeting.

♦ Speak slowly and enunciate.

◆ Use short sentences to quickly get to the point. If other participants are using long statements and grandstanding, interrupt and politely ask them to summarize their key points.

◆ Avoid jargon, colloquial expressions, slang and analogies that non-English speaking participants may not understand. If other participants use these types of speech, ask them to rephrase or restate their points to ensure that everyone understands.

◆ Do not tell jokes. Sometimes jokes are language-specific and when the words are literally translated into another language, they could lack meaning or worse yet—be offensive! Don't go overboard and eliminate all humor or fun, but do take special effort when preparing for the meeting to bridge any gaps that may result from language or cultural differences.

◆ Use visual aids and written documents to reinforce the verbal messages that you or others are communicating during the meeting. For example, use presentation software to display information, graphs, charts, agendas, a list of topics, or issues. Be sure to list ideas, issues, or problems generated by the group on flipcharts or other visual media so that all participants can see what others have communicated.

◆ Observe the nonverbal cues of everyone in the group for signs of lack of understanding. If you think that some participants are lost or do not fully understand the key points, use this as an opportunity to rephrase or summarize what has been said.

◆ Avoid asking if everyone "understands." Participants— even though they may not understand—are often very hesitant to admit that they are lost because they do not want to appear incompetent. Instead, watch for the cues and rephrase items as needed.

◆ Brush up on cultural implications and how to break down barriers when communicating with non-English-speaking participants or those whose primary language is not English. You might want to provide other participants with best practices, articles, or information on how to best communicate within a multicultural group.

Keep the Meeting on Track

Being on track in a meeting means that the group is progressing toward accomplishing the agreed-upon goal(s). That doesn't mean that the group needs to strictly follow the agenda minute by minute. As a meeting leader, you need to allow the group enough latitude for creative discussions, brainstorming, activities, and healthy disagreements as long as they are helping to achieve the stated outcomes. When trying to determine whether to let a discussion continue or if you need to redirect the group in another direction, consider the following guidelines:

- Review the agenda and determine if the time constraints allow for more discussion time or if you need to intervene.
- Review the ground rules regarding discussions that aren't relevant to the agenda and achieving the session objectives. If the discussion is relevant, but throwing the agenda timing off, ask the participants if they want to continue with the discussion (at the sacrifice of something else), or if the discussion should be tabled until another time to remain on schedule.
- Assess why the group has gone off track. Confirm that the group members are clear about the session goals.
- Point out the agenda and remind the group of what needs to be accomplished and help them to understand the time requirements. If needed, bring them back to the appropriate step in the process.
- If one person is getting sidetracked, ask him or her to explain how the item being discussed links to the topic or objectives to try to get the conversation back on track.

STEP 8

◆ Point out your unbiased observations—for example, say, "It seems that some of you are greatly concerned about the current plan for how the new policies will be communicated to the sales representatives." Try to uncover the core issue and get the group back on track with the topics and the agenda—or get the group to agree on what item(s) come off the agenda if more time is to be spent on the current topic.

Gain Agreement

Before ending the session, gain agreement and commitment from participants. Be sure to end the session with the group agreeing on the content and outcome of the meeting. In addition, each participant should make a commitment to further action and should be able to state what he or she is going to do and when.

Conclude the Meeting

It is just as important to conclude a meeting effectively as it is to have a good introduction. The conclusion of a meeting should maintain the enthusiasm that the participants have experienced up to this point.

There are a variety of ways to conclude a meeting and accomplish the final objective of enthusiasm. Some speakers or meeting leaders like to tell a funny story that may be related to the objectives of the meeting. If it's a funny story effectively told, it may well send people away with a smile or a laugh. However, the conclusion of the meeting should do more than that. It should send people away with a feeling of satisfaction that their time and energy were well spent. Depending on the type of meeting, participants should leave with a feeling of accomplishment, achievement, contribution, and importance. As you conclude the meeting, consider the following best practices:

End the session with a memorable message and a feeling of accomplishment. Don't just end the meeting with "well that's it . . . " or "that's all that I have to say . . . " The close of the meeting doesn't need to be long, but it should be memorable and provide a summary of the key points and the expectations for follow-up to action items and next steps. Point out what was accomplished during the meeting, for example, "Great job! We accomplished all of the meeting objectives today ahead of schedule!" so that participants walk away with a sense of the value they provided and the productivity of their efforts.

- ◆ restate the objectives of the meeting
- ◆ summarize what was accomplished
- ◆ thank participants for their contribution (problem-solving, information-getting, attention, and interest)
- ◆ give assignments to one or more persons
- ◆ tell them the time, place, and objectives of the next meeting
- ◆ give final announcements such as, "The meeting minutes will be sent out by tomorrow at the close of business" or "The next meeting will be held next week at the same time" or "Remember to tell your peers and subordinates what we discussed today."

You should avoid ending meetings with "We have time for one more question" (this could open a can of worms and end the meeting on a sour note or push off the meeting's end time by 15 minutes). The meeting should end on a positive note and a reminder that the objectives have been accomplished. There is nothing wrong with having a question-and-answer session at the end of the meeting—just don't end the meeting that way.

You have reviewed the key points necessary to conduct a fast-paced, goal-oriented meeting. Use Worksheet 8.1 to verify that you have considered all the items necessary to lead a successful session.

Now that we've reviewed the key aspects to consider when conducting productive meetings, there is one more consideration to prepare for—how to handle sticky situations and participants whom one might call "prickly pears." Successful meeting leaders are skilled at handling both adeptly to ensure that the meeting progresses and that the goals are accomplished.

WORKSHEET 8.1
Effective Meetings

An effective meeting requires adequate preparation. The amount of time it takes to prepare varies widely and depends on the amount of material that must be researched or gathered, the length of the meeting, current knowledge and familiarity with the meeting topics, previous speaking experience, the type and number of visual aids, and previous knowledge of the audience. To help you prepare for each of these considerations, use the master checklist on this worksheet.

	Presentation Element	Notes
Introduction		
❏	What do you plan to do to welcome the group, warm up the group, and gain their attention?	
❏	What is the subject matter for the meeting? Why was it selected?	
❏	What are the goals and objectives of the meeting? What is to be accomplished and what should participants gain from it?	
❏	Explain how the achievement of the objectives will benefit the participants.	
❏	Describe the points you'll cover in the meeting and their importance to the participants?	
Body		
❏	How do you plan to best communicate or facilitate the points of the meeting?	
❏	How do you plan to capture the participants' interest? Use the following to confirm that your meeting agenda and planned discussions are on target: ◆ Is the language clear and simple? ◆ Will the language be understood by the entire group? Are there any terms or jargon that need to be defined? ◆ What examples will help to relate the points of the meeting?	

(continued on next page)

STEP **8**

Presentation Element	Notes

Outline

☐	◆ Do your notes and agenda include enough detail to illustrate examples you need to communicate key points? ◆ Are the notes in a format that enables you to have more eye contact with participants rather than speaking directly from notes?	

Visual Aids

☐	Are flipcharts: ◆ Printed large enough for all participants to see? ◆ Simple, displaying only key words? ◆ Positioned so that you can stand sideways when presenting? ◆ Appropriate with regard to color, arrows, underscores, circles, and so on for emphasis?	
☐	Are presentation software slides: ◆ Clear and uncluttered? ◆ Formatted consistently (for example, colors/themes)? ◆ Creative with pictures or charts to easily communicate key information? ◆ Structured to reveal only one line at a time so that participants cannot read ahead? ◆ Available in hardcopy format to allow participants to take notes?	
☐	Are handouts: ◆ Available so that every participant has a copy? ◆ Numbered (if there are more than three pages)? ◆ Structured to allow white space for note-taking?	

STEP 8

Presentation Element	Notes

Conclusion

☐ Does the conclusion:
- ◆ Summarize or review the key points?
- ◆ End on a high note that emphasizes what you want participants to remember or take away from the meeting?
- ◆ Provide any suggested reference materials or resources (if applicable) for participants who are interested in finding out more?
- ◆ Review the action items and participants assigned to tasks?
- ◆ Confirm the timeframes for completing action items?
- ◆ Thank the group members for their time and participation?

NOTES

_____

_____

_____

_____

_____

_____

_____

_____

_____

_____

_____

_____

_____

_____

_____

_____

_____

_____

_____

_____

_____

_____

_____

STEP
8

Manage Difficult Situations and Participants

Any time a group forms, many additional group dynamics may influence the effectiveness and productivity of a meeting. Organizational cultures, norms, the size of the group, whether it is a formal or informal meeting, and the type of leadership all play into the mix. So how do successful meeting leaders navigate this potential mine field? They understand how groups form and skillfully manage difficult participants and sticky situations.

So how do meeting leaders identify behaviors that enhance or hinder group effectiveness? They pay particular attention by observing the group and interactions.

Facilitators listen actively throughout the meeting. They observe who spoke; exactly what was said verbatim; how long the members spoke; whom individuals look at when they speak; who supports whom; any challenges to group leadership; as well as non-verbal communication, side conversations, and nonparticipation. They wait for individual reactions to what is being said to help guide and coach the group. Facilitators may ask questions, restate what has been said, summarize positions, or reflect a speaker's feelings. They may also keep track of the different roles group members play.

Stages of Team Development

Teams often generate a tremendous amount of positive energy when they are first formed. Team members are excited, motivated, and ready to roll up their sleeves and tackle tasks immediately. As individuals join together, the team takes on a new life of its own. It will even go through periods of development comparable to the stages of individual growth: infancy, childhood, adolescence, adulthood, and old age. Each phase has its own characteristics and requirements, which build on the ones that come before.

Although the stages of team development are sequentially predictable, each team is unique in how it progresses and regresses through these phases. Some periods of group development can be more painful than others; sometimes teams get stuck at a particular point and cannot advance. One model of group development proposed by Bruce Tuckman and Mary Jane Jensen (cited in *Infoline* 9407, pp. 1–2) identifies the following five stages:

- ◆ **Forming**—During this period, group members tend to be extremely polite. They seek guidance and may be reluctant to participate. Serious topics and personal feelings are avoided. At this stage, the team needs to get acquainted and share personal information. Members should explore similarities among themselves and orient themselves toward the task they've been assigned to address. To grow from this level to the next, team members must be willing to confront threatening topics and risk the possibility of conflict.

- **Storming**—During this stage, boundaries are tested and power struggles or conflicts may develop. Cliques may form. Some members may remain silent, whereas others attempt to dominate. To grow from this point to the next, team members must be willing to give up personal preferences in favor of the requirements of the total group. The team members need to listen, be nondefensive, confront others in a positive way, and be willing to influence and be influenced. Keep in mind that not every conflict is an indication of storming—conflict can be healthy!

- **Norming**—When teams move from storming to norming, they begin merging into a cohesive group (there is more cooperation and understanding). The team has negotiated roles, successfully manages differences of opinion, develops both written and unwritten rules or norms, recognizes the need for interdependence, and masters decision-making mechanics. The team is now ready to tackle the task. Unfortunately, many teams do not make it to this phase. If a team has not established positive relationships during its early stages, or if conflict remains unresolved, these factors will impede the team's ability to make effective decisions.

- **Performing**—The move from the norming to the performing stage is characterized by a high level of trust. Members are recognized for, and encouraged to use, their unique talents. Paradoxically, when a team is highly cohesive and long lived, it is also susceptible to "group think." Group think occurs when individual members suppress their objections and criticisms of others' ideas so that the team can reach agreement with minimal conflict. As a result, the team will make riskier, less-thoughtful decisions. Meeting leaders can help teams avoid group think by helping teams recognize the value of differing and unique opinions and explaining that for the team to succeed, it is important that everyone share his or her opinion with the team—especially when in the minority or when expressing dissenting views.

◆ **Adjourning**—During this last stage, the team prepares for termination. Teams may disband because their work is completed or because team members no longer feel challenged by the task.

How to Manage Difficult Participants

POINTER

When dealing with difficult participants, focus on behavior. Resist the temptation to focus on a specific individual's personality or attitudes as the "bad apple that spoiled the bunch." It is easier to intervene and effectively manage the behavior of an individual than to change his or her personality or attitudes.

So what do you do in the middle of the meeting when someone goes off on a tangent that causes all participants to cast looks of confusion around the room? What do you do when two participants consistently have their own side conversations that cause a low murmur to distract others around the room? What about when one person consistently tries to dominate the conversation—or worse, interrupts every time other participants try to voice their opinions? What do you do when participants are cell-phone junkies or are addicted to their "crack-berries?"

These "prickly pear" types of participants are classic cases of dysfunctional behavior. How you handle the situation can make the difference between losing control of the meeting or tactfully quashing the behavior to guide the group back on track to an effective meeting conclusion. Review the list of situations (see Table 9.1) that may force you to lose control and consider the suggestions for getting the meeting back on track.

STEP **9**

TABLE 9.1
Loss-of-Control Situations and Solutions

What Happens?	Why?	How to Handle
Participant makes a comment or asks a question that is off topic.	Objective is not clear or participant intentionally gets off topic to discuss his or her "burning platform."	Goal: You need to make the participant and the group comfortable and regain control. Consider saying: • "I guess I haven't made the objective clear . . . " • "How does your comment for X tie in with the objective of Y?" • "That's a good comment (or question), but it's a little off topic. Can we discuss it after the meeting?"
Side conversation takes place between two participants.	Something in the meeting stimulated their conversation or they are bored and disinterested and the conversation is off topic.	Goal: Assume the side conversation is about the subject. Give them the benefit of the doubt and maintain a positive attitude. Consider: • Pausing for a few seconds. Silence may shorten their conversation. Look at your notes, take a sip of water, and so on. • Asking them directly if they would like to share their ideas—but communicate it with the assumption that they are discussing something related to the meeting.
Participants are distracted.	Distraction is a major issue for any meeting participants—even though they may be very interested in the meeting. They could also lack interest in the meeting.	Goal: Handle as if all of the meeting participants are distracted or disinterested. Sometimes distractions can be avoided if meetings are held at the proper place and time. Consider: • Stopping the meeting and recognizing the distraction. Don't try to compete with it. • Perhaps suggest a five-minute stretch break or introduce an energizer to interject some fun and then refocus the group. • If a small group is consistently distracted, the leader may choose to ignore their lack of attention or summarize what has been decided in the meeting to try and rein in everyone.

(continued on next page)

What Happens?	Why?	How to Handle
Two or more participants argue with each other.	Something in the discussion is causing off-topic arguments.	Clarify objectives and topics to prevent arguing. Quote Peter Drucker, who states, "It's not who is right, but what is right that is important." Consider: • Stating that all opinions and views are important, but that we need to be willing to listen to and consider the ideas of others. • Concentrating on thoughts presented, not on the people who presented them. • Halting the meeting, revisiting the objectives, and refocusing the meeting and all discussions on accomplishing goals.

The most difficult aspect of conducting productive meetings is keeping the group under control. Successful meeting leaders excel in their knowledge of control approaches, quick thinking, and possess a lot of tact. The best way to control a meeting is to prevent it from getting out of hand. This is often achieved by careful preparation on the part of the leader. For example, if the meeting leader things that one participant may dominate to the detriment of the meeting effectiveness, the leader can talk to the participant prior to the meeting to prevent the domination from taking place.

POINTER

If the disruptive behavior exhibited during a meeting is clearly addressed in the ground rules, remind the group of the agreed-upon rules and adhere to them.

When to Intervene

So when is it appropriate for a meeting leader to intervene? When a discussion veers off course, the meeting leader needs to provide proper feedback and at times alter what the group is doing. The ground rules established at the start of the meeting provide one set of agreed-upon behaviors expected by the group. Therefore, participants displaying behavior counter to those ground rules are most likely showing ineffective behavior. So meeting leaders should intervene to shift the focus of a process to

◆ cause the team to examine its dynamics and improve its performance
◆ encourage member participation
◆ encourage problem solving and decision making
◆ ensure compliance with procedures, policies, ground rules, and requirements that define the process within the organization.

How to Intervene

Successful meeting leaders tactfully intervene in group discussions and ineffective dynamics or behaviors by mastering the following techniques:

POINTER

Don't jump to conclusions! If you see group members displaying what you might consider to be disruptive behavior (for example, side conversations or doodling on paper), give them the benefit of the doubt. For example, side conversations might truly be about the meeting topic with two team members pondering a point to bring up to the group. Many participants learn and process information best when they are "active." These individuals are known as kinesthetic learners and they often need to be doing something with their hands to do their most creative thinking! Perhaps provide pipe cleaners or putting doodle sheets or other fun, tactile items in the center of meeting tables to engage folks and get their creative ideas flowing!

STEP 9

◆ **Describe process obstacles**—if nothing is happening, describe the next step and perhaps encourage the contributions from several participants.

◆ **Encourage participation**—at the start of the meeting, encourage participation and plan activities to maintain participation throughout the session.

◆ **Use body language**—move closer to the table or particular participants to either support those who are under fire or quiet down disruptive members.

◆ **Discourage personal attacks**—by reminding individuals and the group of the ground rules and refocus the discussion on the issue to dissuade personal attacks.

◆ **Suggest a break**—to end a deadlock or simply reenergize the group. Refreshment breaks are common, but others work just as well, such as moving to small breakout groups for a few minutes or taking a five-minute joke break.

◆ **Summarize**—any problem and any alternatives that the group generated. Groups may get lost in discussion and summarizing helps the group refocus and keep moving.

◆ **Present a straw man**—by developing (or suggesting that someone develop) a draft problem description or solution during a break. A straw man encourages the group to criticize the plan, attack it, pull it apart.

◆ **Act stupid**—to help participants who are uninvolved or may not understand what is happening or what someone is saying. These participants may not want to volunteer their ignorance. By asking for clarification of issues, problems, terminology, or anything else that may get in the way of consensus later in the process you can keep participants focused.

◆ **Get specific**—to help clear up hard-to-grasp issues, problems, and solutions.

Strategies to Resolve Conflicts

The phrase "managing conflict" may be a bit of a misnomer when leading meetings. The fact is, conflicts are characteristic of meetings, and effective teams often expect them—and in fact even welcome them to ensure that the group is having a healthy discussion and airing all ideas and proposing solutions.

If conflicts are defined as differences or disagreements, then they are a natural part of group work and meeting processes. However, meeting leaders must skillfully walk a fine line to encourage conflict and opinions while avoiding destructive conflict and behaviors. When managing and resolving conflicts, consider these guidelines:

◆ communicate the process of how an activity or discussion is going to work during the meeting, and then guide the participants in following the process

◆ break problems or issues down into smaller, more manageable pieces to get into a detailed level or discussion and analysis

◆ be supportive, encouraging, and look for shared goals and win–win situations

Encourage active, unbiased listening. At times, what seems to be a conflict is in fact not a conflict at all—rather, it is a breakdown in communication. When this happens, pause and rephrase what you believe you understood from a participant or several participants to clarify all views. This not only benefits you as the team leader but also the rest of the participants who will better follow the discussion and develop a clearer understanding of the positions of other group members. This is a key step in resolving conflict.

- actively listen to participants' views and pose open-ended questions for them to drive the conversation and ideas to a deeper level
- clarify, sort, and value differences—don't try to gloss over, minimize, or deny them
- gain commitment to change attitudes and modes of communication when necessary
- openly praise group members who are willing to suggest new and different approaches; clarify alternatives and avoid jumping to a single solution or answer too quickly
- analyze why conflicts keep occurring—usually participants aren't fighting about what they say they are fighting about
- encourage individuals to take the initiative to change personally
- model the kind of behavior that shows a comfort level with conflict.

When possible, encourage the use of "I" statements rather than "you" statements to depersonalize conflict. Using "I" statements means turning statements from accusations ("you did . . . ") into statements of fact or personal feeling ("I felt this way when this happened . . . "). Depersonalizing a conflict involves looking at a problem objectively.

Worksheet 9.1 offers some common types of disruptive behavior coupled with strategies to employ when you encounter these problems with meeting participants.

With a meeting now skillfully planned and cleverly facilitated, the next step in the process includes effectively wrapping up the meeting, evaluating successes and areas for improvement, and following up on postmeeting responsibilities.

WORKSHEET 9.1
Preparing to Deal with Disruptive Behavior

In an effort to use what you've learned from this step, use this worksheet to apply this information to your meetings and to deal with difficult participants or behavior.

Instructions:

1. In the left column, identify disruptive behaviors that you will likely encounter during a meeting.
2. Put an X in the space next to the action(s) you plan to use to deal with disruptive behavior.
3. Add any additional actions you could use in the blank space provided.

Disruptive Behavior	Action You Plan to Take
Side conversation	☐ Behave as if you know the side conversation is meeting-topic related and ask the participants to add their thoughts.
	☐ Slowly move to the part of the room where the disrupters are and continue the discussion.
	☐ Change the pace of the activity; do something active (have participants get up and brainstorm ideas in groups on flipcharts, and so on).
	☐ Rearrange groups.
	☐ Revisit the meeting ground rules at the start of the next topic.
	☐ Other
Talks too much; monopolizes discussion	☐ If he/she is on the meeting topic, summarize his or her point then ask others what they think.
	☐ Avoid contact with him/her for a while.
	☐ If he/she is off target, say, "Great point, but it is beyond the scope of the meeting topics . . . Let's talk about this offline."
	☐ Put his/her issue on a "parking lot" flipchart.
	☐ Change the pace of the activity and have participants work individually for a period of time.
	☐ Other

Disruptive Behavior	Action You Plan to Take
Complains; is negative about the meeting or the organization	☐ Ask if others feel the same way. If they don't, then offer to listen to him/her during break. ☐ If others do feel the same way, facilitate a "productive tangent." ☐ Acknowledge the complaint, then turn group discussion to strategizing how to overcome it. ☐ If valid, incorporate it into the agenda. ☐ Other
Daydreams; not really "in the meeting"	☐ Change the current activity to make it more active/involving. ☐ If the daydreaming is organization-related and more than one person is doing it, acknowledge it and allow a short discussion, then move on. ☐ Talk to him/her privately during a break and ask how the meeting could be improved to meet his/her needs. ☐ Frequently link the meeting topics to the job. ☐ Other
Challenges the meeting leader or facilitator on content or technique; "know-it-all"	☐ Give the person the spotlight for a few minutes. ☐ Turn the exchange into a discussion by implying that there are multiple points of view and all should be addressed. Ask for other opinions from the rest of the group. ☐ Other
Silent; doesn't participate	☐ Create opportunities for him/her to participate safely in pairs or small groups. ☐ Pace some activities so there is reflection time included before participants discuss and share opinions. ☐ If you can tell by his/her body language that he/she is engaged, listening, reacting, and thinking, consider simply leaving him/her alone. ☐ Other

(continued on next page)

Disruptive Behavior	Action You Plan to Take
Goes off on tangent; misses the point	❏ Find one thing to agree with in what he/she has said.
	❏ Affirm and compliment his/her effort to stay engaged with the content.
	❏ Say, "That would be a logical assumption; however, the truth is . . . "
	❏ If his/her effort is contrived to see what you will do, the most effective behavior is to address the content of the question rather than take the bait.
	❏ Other

Evaluate Your Success and Follow Up

OVERVIEW

Evaluate the meeting

Conduct a self-evaluation

Distribute meeting notes and track commitments

Host a productive meeting

With the meeting nearly closed, the age-old question looms: "How can we tell if the meeting was effective?" Is success based on how much fun the participants had during the meeting? Although having fun might be a characteristic of a productive meeting, it isn't a key metric of success.

Evaluate the Meeting

Evaluating how productive the meeting was should be measured against these criteria:

- ◆ Were the meeting objectives accomplished?
- ◆ Was the meeting held in a time-efficient manner?
- ◆ Were the participants satisfied with the results?

Given the amount of time that people spend in meetings, isn't it surprising how seldom the effectiveness of a meeting is measured? Some meeting leaders periodically distribute evaluation forms to maintain and improve meeting quality. Because many organizations and departments evaluate and focus on improving everything else—why not do the same for meetings?

STEP 10

As a best practice, consider distributing an evaluation form (see the example in Tool 10.1) at the end of a meeting. If you are holding regularly occurring meetings, such as weekly project status updates, distribute the form only once every four meetings to solicit periodic feedback from the group to ensure that meeting quality maintains a high standard.

Conduct a Self-Evaluation

Keep in mind that the point of evaluating a meeting is continuous improvement and maximizing participant time to achieve productivity. The evaluation process not only happens by having the group critique themselves—but some of the most successful leaders learn more by critiquing their own skills and identifying areas of improvement.

After the meeting ends, you can reflect back on the meeting and how the reality compared with what you planned. When conducting a self-evaluation, be careful to be objective and evaluate what happened from an outsider's perspective. The goal is improvement for future meetings! To facilitate this process, consider using the form found in Tool 10.2.

TOOL 10.1
Group Evaluation of a Meeting

Meeting Evaluation

To:

From:

Date:

Title/subject of meeting:

Date of meeting:

1. Did the meeting achieve its objectives?

2. Was time managed effectively?

3. How well did the meeting leader manage interpersonal relationships? What could be improved?

4. What aspects of the meeting could have been better?

STEP 10

TOOL 10.2
Self-Evaluation of a Meeting

A. **Objectives**
  1. What were the meeting objectives?

  2. Were they accomplished?

     ❐ Yes   ❐ No   ❐ Not Sure

  3. Which objectives were not completely accomplished?

  4. Why not? (Be specific.)

B. **Time**
  1. Were objectives accomplished in minimum time?

     ❐ Yes   ❐ No   ❐ Not Sure

  2. If objectives were not accomplished in minimum time, why not? (Be specific.)

C. **Participants**
  1. In your opinion, how satisfied were participants with the meeting?

     ❐ Very Satisfied   ❐ Satisfied   ❐ Dissatisfied   ❐ Very
                                                          Dissatisfied

D. **If I were conducting the meeting again, what would I do the same? What would I do differently?**

	Same	Different	Comments
Location			
Scheduled time			
Selection of participants			
Objectives			
Room setup			
Audiovisual aids			
Agenda			
My own preparation			
Advance notice to participants			
Introduction			
Amount of participation from the group			
Conclusion			

What else would I do differently?

Distribute Meeting Notes and Track Commitments

Can you evaluate how productive the meeting was after you (and everyone else) leave the room? Not always. If action items were decided on in the meeting, the proof of productivity is in participant follow-though.

Often, with so much happening during a meeting, it is easy to forget that the rubber meets the road after the meeting when participants are supposed to be following up on and completing assigned action items. The work completed between meetings is critical to keeping the project moving forward. For that reason, make sure that every action item, its assigned owner, and timeframe for completion are documented and are clearly understood by the individuals tasked with the items.

In fact, the close of the meeting and follow-up on action items is mission-critical for the group to continue to make progress toward the goals outside of meeting hours. After a meeting, don't forget to

- Type up and distribute the notes from the meeting. Make sure that everyone who attended the meeting receives a copy as well as anyone affected by the outcomes of the meeting but who did not attend.

- Plan to follow up on the commitments. If you said that you were going to do something—make sure that you do it in a timely manner!

- Plan a follow-up meeting to make sure that commitments are being upheld and the purpose of the meeting is achieved. Follow-up meetings often point out if any new problems have surfaced that meeting participants need to solve.

- Consider using spreadsheets or tables to capture all of the action items decided in a meeting with the names of those assigned to each task. Many project teams have midweek check-in points during which they update a shared document of tasks to include the status (not started, in progress, completed) of action items, any obstacles or barriers, any new target completion dates, and so on. Often the task status is color-coded (for example, red—not started and behind schedule, yellow—in progress, green—completed).

Worksheet 10.1 provides a handy form to summarize meeting objectives and the tasks generated by the meeting to remind attendees of their commitments.

On a final note, learning how to successfully lead meetings takes practice. Practice improves performance under two conditions:

- You practice the right things.
- You are being critiqued, coached, and helped to improve.

Obviously, the first condition requires the meeting leader to know the elements of a productive meeting. The second condition requires critical analysis of meetings to suggest ways to improve. On your journey of crafting engaging, effective, and productive meetings, continue to looks for ways to improve. As the meeting leader, you must provide the desire. As the old saying goes, "You can lead a horse to water, but you can't make it drink!"

POINTER

If individuals do not complete their action items as assigned, be sure that they follow up with you prior to the next meeting to provide a status of the item, reasons for not completing the agreed-upon item, and the next steps needed for completion, as well as any consequences. Offer to provide help, resources, or other support to accomplish the tasks to keep the group progressing toward their end goals.

Host a Productive Meeting

Your goal is to run a productive meeting. So how do you know if a meeting is productive or not? Something didn't hit the mark if the participants walk away grumbling about a waste of time versus being energized about the task at hand. Well-executed meetings produce ideas and solutions to problems that might not occur to a lone worker at a desk. They boost morale and organizational productivity by creating a feeling of involvement among participants. All of this is accomplished during a time-efficient session, not necessarily short, but always as short as possible to accomplish the meeting goals.

WORKSHEET 10.1
Meeting Follow-Up

After meetings, document the decisions reached and any action items and owners assigned in a follow-up worksheet. These assignments and information should be confirmed in writing and distributed to the persons involved.

Follow-Up Summary Worksheet

From: (name of meeting leader or note-taker)

To: (names of participants and others who should receive the summary listed alphabetically by last name).

Date:

Subject: (meeting topic)

Date of Meeting:	Times: (start and ending)

Location:

In Attendance: (alphabetical list of participants by last name)

Meeting Objectives:
   1.

   2.

Accomplishments:

Assignments:

Additional Comments:

Date of Next Meeting:

Time:	Place:

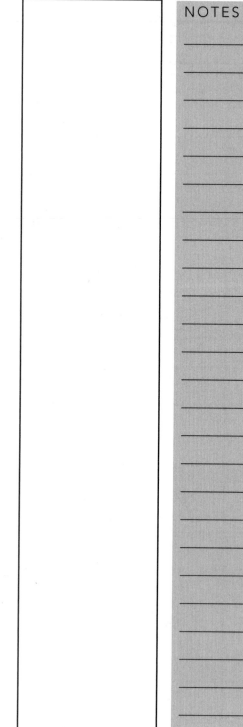

NOTES

C O N C L U S I O N :

Continuing Your Journey

Following the *10 Steps to Successful Meetings* is just the start of your journey in learning how to plan and lead effective, productive meetings. Now that we've gone through the basics, there's still much to learn and additional ways for you to continue to hone and perfect your meeting leader, presentation, and facilitation skills. The following actions are suggested to help you continue to develop your skills:

◆ **Join Toastmasters**—If presentation skills are your Achilles' heel, consider joining Toastmasters—an organization that helps members to improve their ability to speak in public and gain leadership skills in a supportive environment. Meetings are held throughout the country and individuals have an opportunity to make presentations to other members and receive their feedback.

◆ **Take a Communications Course**—Most colleges and many continuing education schools offer classes that teach effective presentation skills. Often they mix practice with theory and are an excellent way to get feedback from both a professional (the instructor) and colleagues.

◆ **Become a Volunteer**—Many organizations look for volunteers to help conduct or lead meetings. What better way to practice your communication and meeting facilitation skills while helping to make a difference for a cause that you believe in?

◆ **Videotape Yourself**—Seeing is believing. Nothing helps meeting leaders to improve their abilities more than watching themselves in action! If you plan to videotape yourself, be sure to get the permission of the meeting participants and explain that it is meant to help you improve your skills and will be kept confidential.

◆ **Read Books and Articles**—Many excellent books and articles have been written on the subject of how to facilitate and lead productive meetings.

◆ **Take a Class**—If you feel challenged by technology, a great way to learn about presentation software is to take a class. Many courses are now available online as well as in traditional classrooms, which should help you to meet your timeframes and schedule constraints.

◆ **Find a Mentor**—A mentor or another seasoned professional who excels at leading productive meetings can be an invaluable tool in advancing your development. Sit in on his or her meetings, and pick the mentor's brain for tips and tricks he or she has learned to successfully manage not only the meeting environment but participants as well.

BIBLIOGRAPHY

Bedrosian, M. (reprinted 1995). "How to Make a Large Group Presentation." *Infoline* No. 259102. Alexandria, VA: ASTD Press.

Biech, E., M. Danahy, and B. Drake. (reprinted 1993). "Diagnostic Tools for Quality Control." *Infoline* No. 259109. Alexandria, VA: ASTD Press.

Callahan, M., and C. Russo, eds. (1999) "10 Great Games and How to Use Them." *Infoline* No. 258411. Alexandria, VA: ASTD Press.

Cassidy, Michael. (1999). "Group Decision Making." *Infoline* No. 259906. Alexandria, VA: ASTD Press.

Darraugh, Barbara. (reprinted 2000). "How to Facilitate." *Infoline* No. 259406. Alexandria, VA: ASTD Press.

_____. (reprinted 1997). "Group Process Tools." *Infoline* No. 259407. Alexandria, VA: ASTD Press.

Eline, L. (revised 1997). "How to Prepare and Use Effective Visual Aids." *Infoline* No. 258410. Alexandria, VA: ASTD Press.

Estep, T. (2005). "Meetings that Work!" *Infoline* No. 250505. Alexandria, VA: ASTD Press.

Finkel, C., and A. Finkel. (revised 2000). "Facilities Planning." *Infoline* No. 258504. Alexandria, VA: ASTD Press.

Guillot, T. (2002). "Team Building in a Virtual Environment." *Infoline* No. 250205. Alexandria, VA: ASTD Press.

Jacobson, S. (1994). "Neurolinguistic Programming." *Infoline* No. 259404. Alexandria, VA: ASTD Press.

Kirkpatrick, Donald. (2006). *How to Conduct Productive Meetings.* Alexandria, VA: ASTD Press.

Kirrane, D. (1988). "Be a Better Speaker." *Infoline* No. 258802. Alexandria, VA: ASTD Press.

McCain, D., and D. Tobey. (2004). *Facilitation Basics.* Alexandria, VA: ASTD Press.

Merriam-Webster's Collegiate Dictionary (11th ed.). Springfield, MA: Merriam-Webster.

Piskurich, G. (2002). *HPI Essentials.* Alexandria, VA: ASTD Press.

Prezioso, R. (revised 1999). "Icebreakers." *Infoline* No. 258911. Alexandria, VA: ASTD Press.

Rosania, R.J. (2003). *Presentation Basics.* Alexandria, VA: ASTD Press.

Russo, C.S. (2000). "Storytelling." *Infoline* No. 250006. Alexandria, VA: ASTD Press.

Spruell, G. (revised 1997). "More Productive Meetings." *Infoline* No. 258710. Alexandria, VA: ASTD Press.

Wircenski, J., and R. Sullivan. (1986). "Make Every Presentation a Winner." *Infoline* No. 258606. Alexandria, VA: ASTD Press.

INDEX

Management of difficult situations, participants, 131–44
Materials, organizing, 91–92
Matrix for room setup, 52
Matrixes, 81–82
Meeting follow-up worksheet, 153–54
Meeting time selection, 24
Mentors, 156
Metaphors, in guided discussion, 43–44
Mind mapping, 71
Mirror, practicing in front of, 92
Multicultural communication, 120–23
Multivoting, 79–80

N
Name bingo, as icebreaker, 100–101
Necessity of meeting, 7–16
 decision regarding, 1
 desired outcomes, defining, 9
 meeting, 15–16
 meeting goals, defining, 9
 types of meetings, 10–16
  facilitative meeting, 12
  informational meeting, 10–11
  instructional meetings, 12–13
  problem-solving meeting, 11–12
  team/project kickoff meeting, 10
  training sessions, 12–13
  virtual meetings, 13–14
Nominal group technique, voting, 79–80
Nonstop talker participant, 94
Nonverbal skills, 118–20
Norming, in team development, 133
Notes of meeting, 149–51

O
Open-ended questions, 103–4
Openers, in meeting opening, 35–37
Opening meetings, 33–38
 acquainters, 35
 icebreakers, 34–37
 openers, 35–37
 warm ups, 35
 worksheet, 111–13

Organizing materials, 91–92
Outstanding questions, discussion of, 45

P
Parking lot, 39, 118
Participants
 acting stupid, as tool in dealing with, 139
 agreements from, 45
 angry participant, 94
 automatic doubter, 94
 body language, 138
 breaks, 138
 chatterer, 94
 commitments from, 45
 conflict resolution, 139–41
 describing process obstacles, 138
 difficult, 93–98
 doodler, 94–95
 encouraging participation, 138
 frequent head shaker, 94
 hair splitter, 94
 identification of, 20–23
 interpreter, 94
 interrupter, 94
 intervention, 136–39
 know-it-all, 94
 loss-of-control situations, solutions, 135–36
 management of, 131–44
 nonstop talker, 94
 personal attacks, discouraging, 138
 planning for, 93–98
 point repeater, 94
 specificity, 139
 straw man, 138–39
 summarizing, 138
 worksheet, 142–44
Participation, encouraging, management of difficult situations, participants, 138
Performing, in team development, 133
Personal attacks, discouraging, 138
Pie charts, 107–8
Planning assessment for meeting, 15–16

Text of visual aids, 106–7
Time selection for meeting, 24
Timely beginning, ending of
    meeting, 116–17
Timing of meeting agenda, 19–20
Toastmasters, joining, 155
Tools for facilitation, 67–83
  affinity diagram, 76–79
  brainstorming, 68–69
  dots, 80–81
  fish bone diagramming, 71–73
  five-why technique, 76
  interrelationship diagram, 76–79
  matrixes, 81–82
  mind mapping, 71
  multivoting, 79–80
  pros/cons lists, 82–83
  round robins, 70–71
  sticky note brainstorming, 69–70
  SWOT analysis, 73–76
    external environmental factors,
      75
    internal environmental factors,
      75
  voting, 83
    simple majority, 83
    super majority, 83
  weighted decision tables, 81–82
Topics of meeting, familiarity with,
    90
Training sessions, 12–13

Transitions, 39
Two truths and lie, as icebreaker,
    102
Types of meetings, 10–16
  facilitative meeting, 12
  informational meeting, 10–11
  instructional meetings, 12–13
  problem-solving meeting, 11–12
  team/project kickoff meeting, 10
  training sessions, 12–13
  virtual meetings, 13–14

U
U-shaped configuration room setup,
    53–54

V
Verbal skills, 118–20
Video camera use, 92
Videotaping, 156
Viewpoint diversity, acceptance of,
    40–41
Virtual meetings, 13–14
Visual aids, 106–8
  text, 106–7
Volunteering, 155–56

W
Warm ups, in meeting opening, 35
Weighted decision tables, 81–82
Worksheet, 96–98, 127–29

THE *ASTD* MISSION:

Through exceptional learning and performance, we create a world that works better.

The American Society for Training & Development provides world-class professional development opportunities, content, networking, and resources for workplace learning and performance professionals.

Dedicated to helping members increase their relevance, enhance their skills, and align learning to business results, ASTD sets the standard for best practices within the profession.

The society is recognized for shaping global discussions on workforce development and providing the tools to demonstrate the impact of learning on the organizational bottom line. ASTD represents the profession's interests to corporate executives, policy makers, academic leaders, small business owners, and consultants through world-class content, convening opportunities, professional development, and awards and recognition.

Resources
- *T+D (Training + Development)* Magazine
- ASTD Press
- Industry Newsletters
- Research and Benchmarking
- Representation to Policy Makers

Networking
- Local Chapters
- Online Communities
- ASTD Connect
- Benchmarking Forum
- Learning Executives Network

Professional Development
- Certificate Programs
- Conferences and Workshops
- Online Learning
- CPLP™ Certification Through the ASTD Certification Institute
- Career Center and Job Bank

Awards and Best Practices
- ASTD BEST Awards
- Excellence in Practice Awards
- E-Learning Courseware Certification (ECC) Through the ASTD Certification Institute

Learn more about ASTD at www.astd.org.
1.800.628.2783 (U.S.) or 1.703.683.8100
customercare@astd.org